BAD MOMMY MOMENTS

BAD MOMMY MOMENTS

Celebrating the Days of New Motherhood that SUCK

Cindy Kane

TWO HARBORS PRESS | MINNEAPOLIS

Copyright © 2012 by Cindy Kane.

Two Harbors Press
212 3rd Avenue North, Suite 290
Minneapolis, MN 55401
612.455.2293
www.TwoHarborsPress.com

All rights reserved. No part of this publication may be reproduced, stored in a retrieval system, or transmitted, in any form or by any means, electronic, mechanical, photocopying, recording, or otherwise, without the prior written permission of the author.

ISBN-13: 978-1-938690-28-0
LCCN: 2012946276

Distributed by Itasca Books

Printed in the United States of America

For Mike,
my best friend, my husband,
and the reason I still laugh late into the night.

CONTENTS

Bad Mommy Moments ix
Please Don't x

THE BEGINNING OF THE END
New Position..1
The Top 10 Things That Surprised Me During Delivery..........2
Here We Go..5
What Remains..7
Puttin' on the Sitz..13
I'm Sorry..14
Philandering Potato (I)...15
The Cautionary Tale of a Girl and Her Medela......................21
Wrong Number...25
Crying It Out...29
Dear Evenflo..31
Babies"R"Us...36
What Did I Do Today?...39
The P-Files...43
Please Hold for Sexy..46
Crazy Lady in CVS: Choose Your Own Ending......................48
Mallrats..53

RESURFACING
The Road Taken..60
Now I Lay Me Down to Sleep...61
Autopilot..62
Cyclical Forgiveness..67
Her Hands...68
The Top 10 Reasons Why I Suck at Mommying......................70
Philandering Potato (II)...72
Feeding the One..75

Bacterial Farm 78
MomFriend 80
Little Gifts 83
Standard Operating Procedures 87
Routines, Screams, and Dropping Bombs 91
Denied 93
Bank Robberies and Sunshine 98
Mama's (Still) Here 101
Instead 104
Words 109
Home 110

THE END OF THE BEGINNING
Philandering Potato (III) 120
You/Him 127
Ladybug Rain Boots 130
Him/You 132
Feeties 134
The Top 10 Warning Signs That You Might Be
    Knocked Up Soon 136
I Shot the Chevy 139
Evolution of the Announcement 142

NEXT TIME
Please, Please Don't 149

Acknowledgments 155

BAD MOM•MY MO•MENTS

noun (plural)

1. short periods of time (that feel like eternities) when you do something "bad" that will haunt you for the rest of the day. Or week. Or forever.
2. the fourth stage of labor
    - stage 1: contractions
    - stage 2: delivery of child
    - stage 3: delivery of the placenta
    - stage 4: delivery of selfish behavior, mean words, and miscellaneous mistakes to your offspring, resulting in mom guilt

PLEASE DON'T

Please don't . . .
. . . tell me to "get my sleep now." Babies wake up every few hours. I'll be tired. I get it.

Please don't . . .
. . . ask how dilated I am. We're at Home Depot. And we just met.

Please don't . . .
. . . give me another parenting book. I'm not going to read it. Just like I didn't read the other ten that changed the course of your family.

Please don't . . .
. . . advise me to get on day care waitlists "just in case." I've already told you, I'm staying at home. I've been planning it since I was a kid. I know you had a hard time and I'm really sorry about that, but I'll be fine. Thanks.

Please don't . . .
. . . insinuate that money will be tight. If we waited until we could afford a baby, we'd never have one. Besides, I wouldn't have quit my job if we weren't able to swing it.

Please don't . . .

. . . ask me if I've joined mom groups. Introverts don't do things like that. Besides, being around other moms and their kids makes me tense.

Please don't . . .

. . . tell us to make time for each other. We've been making time for each other for six years. If there's one thing we've got down, it's "making time."

Please don't . . .

. . . stare at my breasts. Just kidding. Go ahead. And you know what? If I squeeze them together and lean forward, they look even bigger.

Please don't . . .

. . . tell me my life is about to change. Of course it is. I wanted it to change. That's why I got pregnant.

THE
BEGINNING OF THE END

NEW POSITION

-----Original Message-----
From: Big Boss
Posted At: Wednesday, 8:26 AM
Posted To: PBS News
Conversation: CK promoted to new position
Subject: CK promoted to new position

We are delighted to announce that CK, formerly of the Program Management department, officially began her new position as Super Mom on Sunday morning when her new boss—The Baby—was born.

The Baby arrived at 8 pounds 13 ounces and 19 3/4 inches long.

Mom, Dad, and The Baby are all doing well.

We will miss CK but we are thrilled about her new position.

Be more informed. Be more connected. Be more PBS.
Become a member of your PBS station today.
www.pbs.org

This e-mail may contain material that is confidential or proprietary to PBS and is intended solely for use by the intended recipient. Any review, reliance, or distribution of such material by others, or forwarding of such material without express permission, is strictly prohibited. If you are not the intended recipient, please notify the sender and destroy all copies.

------End of Forwarded Message (and life as I knew it)

THE TOP 10 THINGS THAT SURPRISED ME DURING DELIVERY

10.) The appearance of my father-in-law in the delivery room with a Louis L'Amour Western under his arm. He left shortly after.

9.) The fact that I had *zero* control in the delivery room. Since when does a woman naked from the waist down have no power?

8.) When the nurse totally ignored my requests and called in the anesthesiologist. *Hello? Natural birthing plan!*

7.) The numb and tingly joy that started five minutes after the nurse ignored me. Who knew having the bottom half of my body shot up with Novocain would feel so good?

6.) The nurse farting while attending to me. For, like, a whole hour. Of course I said something. I mean, c'mon. This was not a firing range. And if I couldn't feel my legs, how was I supposed to move away from her smoking buns?

5.) My husband pointing out that the nurse wasn't farting—I was. But you see, if I couldn't feel my legs, how was I supposed to feel my butt? And if I couldn't feel my butt, how was I supposed to squeeze my cheeks together to keep them from sounding off?

4.) Pushing brown instead of my baby. While my husband was standing next to me.

3.) The nurse changing the birthing pad beneath me like I was a baby. While my husband was standing next to me.

2.) Not crying when I first saw my baby. But crying when I first saw the doughy remains of my stomach.

1.) Realizing that pregnancy wasn't hard. Giving birth wasn't even that hard. The hard part was convincing everyone that I knew what to do next. Especially since everyone else seemed to know exactly what to do with my baby. How to hold her, diaper her, swaddle her, and nurse her with my breasts. Everyone but me.

BABY'S FIRST LIE

At last my birthday is here!
This is me in my very first photograph ever!

The first thing Mommy and Daddy said when they saw me was:

She's so beautiful!

HERE WE GO

They gift-wrapped her in an old dishrag, grayish-white with faded blue-and-pink stripes. Her skin was red and blotchy, caked with bits and pieces of my uterus. They coated her eyes with a clear gel to protect them from bacteria, but she looked like she'd smoked up in my birth canal. Her mouth was wide: a long, dark tunnel.

I glanced at my husband. He leaned over my shoulder, eyeing her. His gaze was so intense that I felt intrusive, even though I was the only one who couldn't leave the room.

"Do you feel it yet?" he said.

"No," I said. "You?"

"No."

The nurse secured our matching ID bracelets and slipped the baby from my arms, assuring us that we'd see her again as soon as the doctor finished the examination.

"So I guess that's that," my husband said.

"Almost," said the midwife, as she spread my legs farther apart. We'd forgotten that she was in the room stitching me back together again.

He leaned in closer and whispered, "Think we'll feel it soon?"

"I hope so," I said. "I mean, I *know* I love her. Of course I love her. It just doesn't . . ."

"Doesn't feel like what you were expecting?"

"Not at all," I said.

"Did the rest of it feel like what you were expecting?"

I looked down. Fluids still dripped into my arm through a procession of tubes dangling from an IV. My body twitched from the fading epidural. My thighs were dead weight. My vagina may or may not have been in the room. I sighed. When the feeling returned to my legs, the midwife helped me to my feet and eased me over to a wheelchair. She grabbed the handles and pushed me away from the bed. My husband gathered our suitcase and scattered belongings. I took one last look around the room, knowing I'd left my old life in there somewhere even though I couldn't see it from the doorway. A nurse closed the curtain behind us and started to clean up.

My husband and I stared down the long hallway together. He kissed the top of my head.

Here we go. . . .

WHAT REMAINS

Squeeeeeeeeze. Release.
Squeeeeeeeeze. Release.
Squeeeeeeeeze. Release.
There I stood.
Feet away.
From the john.
And yet I couldn't hold it in. I'd been not-peeing on myself for twenty-four years, but if I hadn't been swathed in a foot-long maxi pad, my socks would've been soaked. *Why, oh why hadn't I done the Kegels?* Not that it would've been any easier had I made it to the toilet. My uterus was so heavy I feared it would plop in the water if I removed my wrappings. And the pain! It felt like I was squeezing a medieval flail between my thighs. Why had the nurses offered me Percocet? Why couldn't they have just slipped them into the IV I was still dragging around? I could never knowingly accept narcotics. I was breast-feeding.

The bathroom I dragged myself into was triangular-shaped and wallpapered in a fabric similar to the hospital gown falling off my shoulders. Everything was cream. The shelves, the sink, the tiles, the towels. If I took my gown off, I'd blend into the decor. The shelf I needed was right above the toilet and loaded with items that the nurses had recently used to assault my vagina: pain-relieving spray, TUCKS Medicated Pads, maxis the size of shin guards, and a pile of disposable fishnet boxer-panties. All that was missing was the ice glove, which I could ring for when the one melting in my underwear sandwich got warm.

I was almost to the shelf when I caught sight of my reflection in the mirror. My skin was translucent. My freckles were fat from all of the fluids. My eyes were puffy from the pushing. I looked away from the wreckage, and that was when I heard it.

Squeak. Squeak. Swoosh. Squeak. Squeak. Swoosh.

I gripped the sink and prayed for the sounds to disappear.

Squeak. Squeak. Swoosh. Squeak. Squeak. Swoosh.

But they didn't.

Squeak. Squeak. Swoosh. Squeak. Squeak. Swoosh.

The sounds got closer and closer until they stopped in the hall right outside of my door. Panic fluttered up my throat as I scanned the bathroom. What reason could I give Big Nurse for being in the bathroom alone? Was I exploring? Settling in? Attempting to reapply the makeup that had smeared during childbirth? While my brain fought to recall any other activity I could engage in that close to a toilet, my bladder remembered why I was there, and released.

"I *told* you not to try that again," grumbled Big Nurse. "You need to call us *each time* you have to use the bathroom." She reached for my IV stand. I dropped it and backed away. Big Nurse was the size of two small nurses, with a neck lost somewhere in her shoulders. She owned the Recovery Floor, her presence announced by the sneakers-and-scrubs cowbell she wore one size too small. At just the sight of her I relinquished my very last ounce of control. Literally. I peed on myself again, right there in front of her.

She waved Assistant Nurse into the room. "Her epidural hasn't worn off yet, so until I decide she can do this on her own, we're gonna help her." Big Nurse handed the IV stand to Assistant Nurse and added, "Make sure the tubing doesn't get caught on the toilet handle." They ushered me toward the seat and lifted up my gown. Before she permitted me to sit, Big Nurse peeled down my saturated underthings and peeked at my remains.

"You been sitting on those ice gloves like I told you to?"

"Yes."

"Well, you're still swollen, so it's gonna sting when you pee. Little worse this time since you don't want pain meds."

"Good," I said.

"And you won't recognize yourself. So you might want to wait a few days before inspecting your, you know . . ."

"My vagina?" I said. *My poor, sweet, mangled vagina.*

Big Nurse nodded. Assistant Nurse blushed. They'd already seen more of my vagina in daylight than my husband of four years, but calling it by its clinical name made them uncomfortable? I took my time peeing. A little squirt here, a wince. A longer squirt there, two winces. I reached for toilet paper and smiled at Big Nurse. She boxed my hand away from the roll and shoved a fistful of TUCKS at me. I rolled my eyes, but inwardly sighed. The cool white disks were delightfully refreshing.

Once I was reassembled, the nurses led me back to the bed, and heaved me onto the adjustable mattress as my phone began to ring. It was Grammy. I turned off the ringer. Once back against the pillows, I stretched my legs and pulled the blankets up to my neck. The nurses stood there. I turned away and closed my eyes, but they didn't leave.

"Yes?" I said.

Big Nurse pulled the blankets back down. "We'll just be a minute. We need to check your bleeding." She pressed down on my belly and rolled her hands forward, as if trying to get out that last bit of toothpaste. "Okay, put your hands here," she instructed Assistant Nurse. "You wanna push down like this to get the most blood out."

I willed myself to faint. I pictured my vagina from that angle, all swollen and bearlike. Dizziness circled my brain; I held my breath. I hadn't focused this hard since the last time I chased an orgasm.

"When you're done with that, she needs to be checked."

I exhaled. "For what?"

"Hemorrhoids."

"I don't have any hemorrhoids."

"Of course you don't." She turned to Assistant Nurse. "Let's roll her over. You have to make sure they're not bleeding."

I closed my eyes again. At least my husband wasn't here. At least my baby was scheduled to be in the nursery for another hour. At least there was no one else in the room to witness the manhandling of my alleged anal veins.

A baby down the hall wailed. It was loud and mad. I pitied the mother who had to greet that child. My nipples throbbed with pain anyway, as if the raging newborn were going to make a pit stop in my room and attack random breasts. Was this how my body was going to react to every child who cried? Or would my nipples fall off so I'd be free to take Percocet and bottle-feed without guilt? The wheels stopped at my door. I opened my eyes. A third nurse entered, rolling a plastic drawer with the screaming baby in it toward my bed. Closer. Closer. I hadn't even recognized her cry.

"Awww! Sounds like someone's ready for lunch!" Assistant Nurse cooed.

I tried to bury my head in the pillow, but from my angle all I could do was strain my neck.

"Whoa! What's going on in here?" my husband said as he entered the room. I squeezed my eyes as tightly as I could, but I heard the smile on his face. And the clicking of our camera. And the baby's cry. And the squeaking and swooshing of Big Nurse as she herded everyone else toward the door.

Maybe I took the Percocet and was having hallucinations.

Maybe I hadn't given birth yet and this was a dreamlike panic attack.

Maybe I hadn't just peed on myself.

Again.

GETTING STARTED

Welcome to the new, larger BREASTS® included with the post-delivery body. BREASTS® work directly with hungry infants or breast pumps. (See Hardware.) Read on to find out how to get started with the new BREASTS®.

CONNECT BREASTS®

The infant should be brought to the BREASTS® immediately following delivery. The infant generally clamps down on the nipple instinctively, thus connecting itself to the BREASTS®.

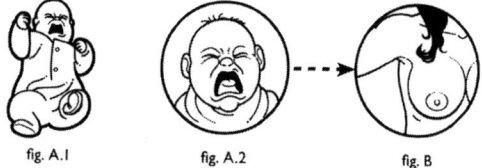

fig. A.1   fig. A.2   fig. B

For some individuals, this process may be devoid of the benefits suggested by doctors and breastfeeding advocates for several reasons:

1. It feels as though the child has <u>barbed wire in its gums.</u>

2. The individual has never used the BREASTS® for this purpose before.

3. The individual may find it hard to focus on the child if the doctor has not concluded the stitching of their vagina.

4. The individual may find it disconcerting to sit half-naked in a highly trafficked room and inquire, "Is it sucking on my nipple correctly?"

5. The individual's placenta is still somewhere close by, probably in a plastic tub.

6. The birthing class did not instruct on how to correctly respond when strangers grab the BREASTS® to feed the infant when the individual fails to make contact.

7. [See also: Reason 1.]

*PLEASE NOTE: Some infants decline connection to the BREASTS®. This is acceptable. Neither the BREASTS® nor the infant are invalid. Our studies have yielded only that these particular infants prefer not to acknowledge warm milk if expressed by means of fleshy tissue. Said infants will continue to grow and develop at a satisfactory pace with formula or milk expressed via the Hardware listed on page 3.

12

PUTTIN' ON THE SITZ

We've had some exciting times over the years, you and I. Different places, different positions, different hours of the day . . . and night. I always preferred the days, as they were easier to navigate, but we found each other in the dark as well, often embracing for hours at a time.

Even still, when the nurse informed me of your involvement in my healing process, I was skeptical. She shrugged, handed me the sitz bath, and instructed me to place it along your rim if things got a little sore "down there." The sitz was an interesting contraption: a plastic, clay-colored tub designed to nestle just inside your seat. Attached to it was an IV bag and some tubing. I thanked her, but had no intention of soaking my "down there" inside of it.

But after being home a few days, the swelling "down there" went away, and the pain it left behind made me waddle like I had a pineapple in my drawers. And drawers they were. There hadn't been a pretty panty in sight since a month before the birth. I feared I might never stand before the Victoria's Secret "5 for $25" table again.

As I put away the last of the baby presents and finally unpacked my suitcase, I found the sitz bath. And I imagined how nice it would feel to take a dip in my toilet spa and feel the eternal spring of hot water bubbles. Perhaps it would bring hope to a very sad and depressed vagina. And as I steeped myself in the clay-colored tub, I understood why the nurse hadn't said much; she didn't need to. A product like this didn't need an introduction. When paired with a Grade A toilet like yourself, in a locked bathroom with the fan on . . . oh, it was glorious.

You always did know my "down there" better than anyone.

I'M SORRY

I'm sorry my bracelet snagged your umbilical nub and ripped it off. I'll never wear jewelry again, I promise.

I'm sorry I placed you into the shaking arms of Great-Grammy. It was like offering a crystal vase to an earthquake (although it helped with your gas problem). I'll never let her hold you again, I promise.

I'm sorry I lost grip of your legs while changing your diaper. Your bottom landed on a terry-cloth changing pad and you slept through the whole thing, but I'll never let go of you again, I promise.

I'm sorry your neck flopped back as I tried to secure the baby carrier. Thank God your head didn't snap off. We'll never use the carrier again, I promise.

I'm sorry you woke up with the cat licking you directly on the mouth. I hadn't planned to ask him to babysit; I just really needed to pee. I'll never get another babysitter, I promise.

I'm sorry you breathed in your own vomit because I was on the phone and didn't notice your nose pressed into the spit-up on my shoulder. I'll never pick up the phone again, I promise.

I'm sorry I left you in the swing all night. You were only supposed to be in there for a few minutes, but you quieted down and then I fell asleep. I can't believe the nurses let me take you home without giving me some sort of written test. I'll never sleep again, I promise.

PHILANDERING POTATO (I)

The doorbell rang at 7 a.m. The dog barked. The baby jumped against my breast.

My God, I thought, *someone found him.*

I placed the baby in her swing and rushed to the front of the house. The dog beat me to the door. I yanked her back by the collar so she wouldn't maul the guest. The dog yelped. The woman backed up. The baby started to cry. I'd forgotten to turn the swing on.

I pushed the dog into the house, closed the door behind me, and turned to the woman on the stoop. She looked vaguely familiar, though I couldn't place her. Petite, dark-haired, somewhere in her fifties, and perfectly attired in Ann Taylor. I was suddenly aware that all I had on was a bathrobe. The same robe I'd put on two days ago, when I last stepped out from the shower.

"Sorry about that," I said. "The dog gets a little excited."

The woman nodded.

"Can I help you?" I asked. The morning breeze felt cold against my damp breasts. The chill caused an involuntary letdown. Milk streamed toward my stomach.

"My name is Annette," she said. A nervous twitter broke her words. She focused her eyes on the door behind me. "I live a few blocks down," she continued. "Your husband stopped by the other day and mentioned that Harry is missing."

"Harry?" I said.

"The cat?"

"You mean . . . oh, right. *Harry*." The cat. I'd named him Harry when we first got him, as I believe it is every screenwriter's duty to name at least one pet after a Gene Hackman character. I had it engraved on a nametag that the cat "lost" several months later when my husband rechristened him "Potato." Since I refused to address my beautiful Maine coon as a starchy, tuberous crop, I never bought him another tag. But I must have started mentally referring to him as Potato because "Harry" now sounded wrong. Or maybe it was her tone, a little too familiar and concerned for a casual glance out the window. Or maybe it was the fact he hadn't worn that tag in over two years. I looked at the woman. She wouldn't meet my eyes.

"We've, I mean, he comes around a lot, and we've grown quite fond of him." She stared down at her leather flats. "We're really worried about how long he's been missing. We've looked for him every day."

"What do you mean, 'he comes around'? He's come into your yard?"

"Well, yes. . . ." She gazed at the rhododendrons.

"You've let him in your house," I said.

"It's not that simple."

"No?"

"We had a cat for fifteen years that we really loved. She had cancer and her oncologist performed surgery and chemo, but she died. We never thought we could love another cat again. And then we met Harry."

"Potato," I said. "His name is *Potato*. You know, as in rhymes with *gato*. Spanish for cat." *Stupid name.*

She finally made eye contact with me. Her mouth dipped into a dainty O.

"We call him Mr. Fluffy," she said.

"I see."

"Anyway, please let us know if you find him. I haven't slept in days."

THE BEGINNING OF THE END

"Right. Sure," I said.

"Thanks."

"You're welcome."

We stood there, arms folded across our chests (although mine were folded to keep my robe closed). I stared at her. Willed her to look at me again. But she smiled at the door and scurried away. She even inspected the holly bushes—our holly bushes—for the cat before crossing the street. I wanted to shove her into them. Instead, I decided to go inside and tell my husband about it. He'd be shocked. We'd take her name in vain. Then we'd find the cat, close off the dog door, and introduce him to his new life as an indoor animal.

I turned the knob. It wouldn't budge. I turned it again, harder this time, and rattled it. Nothing. It was locked.

I'd locked myself outside.

I took a deep breath and rang the doorbell. The dog barked. The baby started to cry. I hadn't even noticed that she'd stopped. I rang the doorbell again, this time with the pulsating force of an SOS. Nothing. I felt tunnel vision coming on. I pounded on the door. The dog howled. The baby wailed. My breasts leaked. Again.

"It's just me, Maggie," I said into the peephole. "Calm down." Maggie growled at the door. How did my husband not hear any of this? I strained my ears and could make out the faint pattering of the shower. I had to get inside before I lost it in the front yard. *In front of her.*

I peered around. Annette was gone. I fled through the gate, toward the back of the house. I grabbed the basement doorknob, but it was locked, too. I looked down at my last option. The dog door. I put my foot through the heavy rubber square just as the dog ran out of it and clipped my knees, knocking me to the concrete. Since I was already on the ground, I crawled through.

17

The crying inside was much louder than I'd thought. I stumbled up the steps and reached the kitchen just as my husband lifted our daughter out of the swing. Silence. I wandered over to the cat's dishes. His food was still untouched. A fly had perished in his water.

"What happened?" my husband asked. He entered the kitchen in a towel, water dripping off of his face. He held the baby in front of him. She'd spit up all over her flowered dress. "How long has she been . . ." His eyes widened as he looked from her to me.

I followed his gaze. Dirt and dust covered the front of my robe, which was open and pushing out skin like a Play-Doh Fun Factory. My melon postpartum panties glowed in the natural light of the kitchen and were big enough to fully clothe our sticky baby. I sunk to the kitchen floor and wept. The dog licked my face until she dried my cheeks. I felt like a leper. My husband took the baby upstairs and returned alone several minutes later. He sat down on the floor and wrapped his bare arms around me. He smelled of fruity hair conditioner. He must have run out of his own again. When was the last time I'd gone shopping?

I curled into his chest and let him rock me. I was determined to mold my thoughts into a coherent string of sentences. I wanted to tell him everything. I wanted us to be angry together. I started with the ringing of the doorbell, and a gross, hiccupy crying followed. "They call him Mr. Fluffy!" was all I managed to wail between gulps. He pulled away from me and closed my robe.

"Shhhh. It's okay," he whispered. "Just admit it and we'll all feel better."

I looked up at him, confused. He stroked my matted hair.

"Potato *was* a pretty awesome name," he said with a smile. "Wasn't it?"

THE BEGINNING OF THE END

BAD MOMMY MOMENTS

USING BREASTS®

Once the milk comes in, the user may experience excitement due to the enormity of the BREASTS®. Read on for tips on using BREASTS®. You can also find information about maintaining and safely exhibiting BREASTS®. (See Learning More, Service and Support.)

Turning breasts on and off
To turn BREASTS® on, attach infant to the nipple. Keep infant awake during each session by removing socks, blankets or by applying ice to exposed appendages. If the infant should fall asleep or become disinterested, the BREASTS® will turn off automatically after two minutes.

To turn the BREASTS® off immediately, press and hold a nursing pad against the nipple for several seconds. (See Hardware.)

HARDWARE (not included)

Nursing pads
Breast Maxi Pads are designed to keep the BREASTS® dry day or night. Disposable pads are thin with a plastic lining to insure that the BREASTS® do not have untimely accidents. They are also available in 100% washable cotton, but this style fills quickly and leaks accordingly.

Lanolin
Use this waterproofing wax to sooth sore and cracked nipples. Apply salve copiously before and after each session to avoid excruciating pain when bringing infant to the BREASTS®.

Electric breast pumps
Be careful when selecting the right pump. Most models are convenient, create sufficient letdown, and collect milk as designed. Others, however, have been reported to function with such aggressive sucking power as to generate bleeding, thus destroying the collected sample.

Earplugs
When the breast pump is in use, consider earplugs for all other individuals in the vicinity, as the pumps often sound like farm equipment.

20

THE CAUTIONARY TALE
OF A GIRL AND HER MEDELA

Raaa-ssss raaa-ssss raaa-ssss raaa-ssss raaa-ssss raaa-ssss raaa-ssss.

The other night I slipped away from our dinner party to pump. The baby had fallen asleep in someone else's arms and since I obsessed regularly about a declining milk supply, it was time for a little one-on-one with my Medela. I left my husband with his family, raced up to the baby's room, and closed the door. By the soft glow of the baby monitor I could see what a hole the room was. Onesies, pj's, and little socks exploded out of the hamper. A leaning tower of diapers balanced atop a wastebasket because I couldn't figure out how to work the Diaper Genie refills. Luckily, people lost interest in seeing the nursery when the baby wasn't in it.

I sat down on the glider and put my big ol' pump case on the ottoman. I pulled down the straps of my tank top and wrestled with the heavy nursing bra. My tremendous breasts plunged out. As a former B girl, double-Ds were a whole new experience. They had weight; if I went one way, they had the option to go the other. They didn't disappear when I took off my bra, and they actually hurt when I ran down the stairs. I loved them. And I spent a great deal of time plotting how to keep them once the baby stopped nursing, even resolving to pump for the rest of my life.

I situated myself in the chair, stuffed my breasts into the cone-shaped shields, and turned on the pump. *Raaa-ssss raaa-ssss raaa-ssss raaa-ssss raaa-ssss raaa-ssss raaa-ssss.* The reviews claimed that this particular model felt "more like baby," but they didn't elaborate on the conducted research. They also neglected to note how many newborns sat still with their mouths wide open to measure for width and comfort. Or whose plastic-faced baby had a dial on its cheek to adjust the painful suction.

I started things slow, dial turned to 2, confident that business would soon conclude. I sat back and waited for letdown. I waited and waited until the sucking motion felt like it was starting to pull the skin off of my already battered nipples. I turned it up a few notches to 5. *Raa-sss raa-sss raa-sss raa-sss raa-sss raa-sss raa-sss raa-sss raa-sss.*

"Aaaaaaaaaaa!" My nipples were going to wind up in the collection container. Frustrated, I pushed the "one-touch letdown" button several times. Ow. Ow. Ow. Nothing. I thought that perhaps a little mental stimulation might help, so I flipped open the top of my microfiber shoulder bag. The Medela included a little plastic sleeve intended for a photograph of the child. I felt a little pervy doing this at first. I mean, do I put in a picture of the kid clothed or in a diaper? Naked? I settled on one of the baby screaming when she was hungry, which usually did the trick. But not tonight. So I adjusted the speed to 10. I'd never gone all the way with my Medela before. But I needed to get back to my husband's family. To Grammy. *Ra-ss ra-ss ra-ss ra-ss ra-ss ra-ss ra-ss ra-ss ra-ss ra-ss ra-ss ra-ss.*

"Oh my God. Oh my God. Oh my God!" I cried out. And just as I reached for the "off" button, I felt my body swell. My breasts tingled and reached for the ultimate relief. "Aaaaaaaaaaaaaaaaaaaaaaaaaa . . ." I smiled in the dark. "Mmmmmmmmmmmmmm . . ." Pain forgotten, I looked down at the white substance filling up the attached bottle. It promised to be at least an eight-ounce escapade. Everything was going to be okay.

And then I heard footsteps thumping up the stairs. I straightened my back and pulled my feet up on the glider so my knees would block the breast shields and the rest of my exposed chest. My husband opened the door. A screech of feedback rushed in with him, magnifying the noise of the pump at least ten times. Then the pumping noise was in stereo; I flipped off the Medela. My husband pointed the antenna of a baby monitor in my face.

"You left this on downstairs," he said. I heard his voice in front of me and also through the receiver in his hands.

Oh.

Oh.

Oh no.

I gasped.

He reached beside me to turn off the base. Static filled the room. "Next time, you might want to bring this upstairs with you. Or just turn it off," he said. He shut it down.

Silence.

"It was on the porch?" I whispered.

"No," he said.

"Under the couch?"

"Nope."

The hum of music and laughter slipped into the room. I dropped my head. I peered down at the collection cups. The milk had stopped and my breasts had shrunken away from the plastic shields. I put the containers on the floor. I would hurt later.

"Don't . . . don't tell me," I said.

"Behind the coffee machine, on the counter."

"Oh, God."

"It took me a good minute to find it."

"Oh, God."

"Yeah, I think we've all heard enough of that tonight." He reached down and offered me his hand. I turned away from him. I was *not* leaving the room.

"You have to," he said. "This party was your idea."

I stood and followed him out of the room. Maybe I could

just keep going and leave the house when we reached the bottom of the stairs. He stopped short. I banged into him.

"What?" I said. "Why did you stop?"

He looked down at my massive breasts.

Seriously? I thought. *Right now?*

"You might want to," he said, "you know . . ."

"No, I don't know. What? What *do you* think I should do?"

He smiled. "Pull your shirt back up?"

Oh.

My nursing bra and tank top were sodden with milk, and hung from my chest like mud flaps. "I'll . . . um," I said. "I'll be, um, down in . . ."

He wrapped me in a hug and kissed the top of my head. He didn't say anything, but I could feel his chest beating with laughter. I gazed up at his face. He looked away. I wrapped my arms around him and hugged him as tightly as I could.

Keep laughing, I thought. He turned and went down the stairs. In the light of the hall I could see two wet spots on his shirt from where I'd rubbed my nipples against his chest.

You just keep on laughing.

WRONG NUMBER

"Hello?" I rubbed my eyes and sat up. The person on the other line hacked up a fistful of phlegm. I pulled the phone away from my ear and turned my head, but it was too late. Her germs slid down the back of my neck.

"Hello?" I asked again. Another gargled cough. I don't know why I bothered posing it as a question. I knew who it was.

"Hi, Grammy."

"Hello? I can't hear anything!"

"HI, GRAMMY."

"Oh, hi-i-i. Is anyone coming out to see me today?"

"YES, WE'LL BE OUT AS SOON AS THE BABY GETS UP FROM HER NAP."

"Is she in a better mood this time?"

"SHE WAS IN A FINE MOOD LAST TIME, GRAMMY. BUT SHE'S A BABY AND . . ."

"Oh, good. I look forward to it. Byyyyyyye."

Click.

I slumped against the pillows and pulled the warm blankets up to my shoulders. I closed my eyes and tried to go back to sleep, but I couldn't stop comparing the items on Grammy's latest list with what I'd purchased. I was sure I'd forgotten something. I should've just kept the piece of envelope she'd written everything on. But I'd been so mad at her for greeting me with a list of things she wanted that I'd tossed her list in the trash when she turned away.

I got out of bed and trudged downstairs. I pulled the plastic bag out of the closet and rummaged through it. Werther's Originals, Ivory Snow soap, a bathmat, table water crackers,

Downy fabric softener in the blue bottle, *Girl with a Pearl Earring*, twenty-four AA batteries, and a note to remember the apricots and Jarlsberg in the fridge.

*

 My cell phone vibrated in my jacket pocket as I clicked the baby's carrier into its base. I looked down at her. She was smiling at me, her eyes intensely locked on mine. I leaned my nose against hers. She sighed and reached out her hands. I wanted to stay right there. My phone beeped with a new message.
 Hello? Hello, are you there? I can't hear you. Well, look, if you can hear me I wanted to make sure you picked up Downy fabric softener, the one in the blue bottle, to use for my delicates. And I'd also like some Ivory Snow soap. That Dove you brought me attracts mosquitos. Okay, thank you. Byyyyyyye.
 Click.
 I pounded my fists on the top of my car. Her car, actually. She'd given me the Cavalier when she could no longer drive. I turned away from it and stared at my house. *Her* house. She agreed to let us live there once she had to move into a nursing home.
 I was angry, but not at her. It wasn't her fault that I'd dismissed my husband's concerns that he wasn't making enough to support us. It wasn't her fault that I'd gotten us waitlisted at only *one* day care. It wasn't her fault that my husband and I fought for two weeks because I wanted him to ask her for money, and he wanted me to get a job. I was still determined to stay home with our daughter, even though I wasn't adjusting and already wanted to return back to work, but couldn't admit it. And it wasn't her fault that she was generous with her money and that, as a result, I was further in her debt. It was my fault. All of it.

For the first fifteen minutes of the drive I created scenarios where she'd yell at me for forgetting whatever it was she wanted, and I'd shoot back about the many tasks she assigned to me each week. I'd emphasize how much I did to keep her happy, and her grandson happy, and her great-granddaughter happy. For the remainder of the drive I stewed in the thankless servitude of washing, folding, and putting away her clean laundry, straightening her kitchen, forcing her to apply hand sanitizer before holding the baby, and then using a pillow to support her frail, trembling arms. Fury burned my thoughts as I imagined having to apologize again and again for the indecency of forgetting the mystery item while she hacked old age all over my new baby. *God*, I thought. *Please get me through this.*

I glanced out my window and noticed a Starbucks. If I armed myself with a coffee, I could handle it. I grabbed my purse and counted the change while watching the light. I had just enough for a . . .

Cappuccino.

She'd wanted a cappuccino.

My spirits lifted as I cut over two lanes of traffic and pulled into the parking lot. I unhooked my daughter and skipped her into the darkened store, inhaling the ground coffee beans and steamed milk. I ordered the cappuccino and smiled. I could do this. It was my mess, and I needed to be an adult about it. And for the very first time I'd actually head into her room with everything she'd asked for. I bounced the baby around the store as we waited for Grammy's beverage. My cell phone vibrated in my jacket pocket. I opened it without checking the number.

"Hello?" I said.

She hacked up a fistful of phlegm. I pulled the phone away from my ear and turned my head, but it was too late. Anxiety shot up my back.

"Hello? I can't hear anything."

"HI, GRAMMY."

"Oh, hi-i-i. Are you on your way? I just wanted to make sure you didn't forget my cappuccino again this week."

"No, I—"

"Because you forgot it the last two times you came. Do you read my lists?"

"Grande extra hot cappuccino?" the barista called from behind the machine. He put the drink down on the counter. I stared at the white cup, steam escaping from the small opening, dissipating into the air. I thought about leaving her drink and going home. I could turn off the phone. Probably even fall back to sleep.

"Hello? Are you still there?"

"I'm getting it right now, Grammy," I whispered.

"Oh, good. I look forward to it. Byyyyyyye."

Click.

CRYING IT OUT

I checked my watch again. It should've been an hour, maybe even two. But according to its smudged face, I'd only been staring outside for fifteen minutes. I glared at the second hand, hating it for the freedom with which it glided around its world. I wanted to move smoothly along, but the cramp in my lower back reminded me that I hadn't moved in forever. Or at least a quarter past forever.

I looked back out the windows and waited for the fog of my nearsighted eyes to lift. I gazed from the blurry grass to the bare trees to the dark clouds smeared against the gray sky. Everything swayed. I wished my ears were as myopic as my eyes, then maybe I wouldn't hear her wails. I put my fingers in my ears and pressed them as hard as I could, but her screams found me.

I wanted to go outside but felt guilty for even considering it. What if she stopped breathing? What if she smothered herself in the bumper? What if she passed out from crying? I'd already spoken with an on-call nurse who assured me she was fine and that there wouldn't always be a reason for crying. But I wanted a reason. Preferably one I could silence with infant Motrin.

The dog came up beside me and nudged my leg. I slid open the heavy door and watched her race down the cement steps after a lone squirrel. She almost caught it. She always came close. Since the door was already open, I grabbed my iPod and slipped outside. The wind flipped my hair behind me. I inhaled the winter until it seized my lungs and made me cough. My body shook. I wrapped myself inside of my sweater and sat down on the cold cement. It felt good to respond to something other than the baby's cries. I was tired of failing to quiet her. I was tired of being so far away from home. I was tired of being tired. I pulled the iPod out of my pocket and popped in the ear buds. Scrolled through some of the louder Beethovens. Decided on the third movement of *Tempest* and smirked at my irony.

  I leaned against the iron railing. Sleety rain speckled my face. I looked up at God hiding behind the thick batting of clouds. He could make it storm if He wanted. I was out and I wasn't going back in. I closed my eyes as the pianist's fingers argued across the keys. I joined the sonata, pounding out my frustration on an imaginary keyboard. And then something swatted my hands. I gasped.

  "Potato!" He climbed into my lap. I rubbed my nose in his fur. He reeked of gasoline. "Were you stuck in someone's garage again?" He nudged into my sweater, shielding himself from the rain. I closed the knitted cords around him and felt his warmth surge through my lap. The baby wailed. The sleet pelted my face. The sound of the piano built to a crescendo. Inside my sweater the cat circled and kneaded my stomach into a nest. I hugged him close, gazed up at the baby's window, and smiled.

DEAR EVENFLO

Dear Evenflo:

When I registered for a baby monitor, I chose your Whisper Connect series because of the rechargeable batteries, the range of sound and, most importantly, the "soundlights." I loved the idea that I could watch the red lights dance across your product in response to my child's sweet little bed activities several rooms away.

Your product worked better than I dared to hope. Even at the quietest setting it picked up every single sound she made and nudged me out of sleep or my "me time" to alert me of her needs. Little by little the Whisper Connect series became such an intricate part of my life that I couldn't turn it off. I needed to know *exactly* what was happening in my child's room every moment she was in there. I measured my success at mothering by the noises that came from the speakers. And even when I had the strength to turn off the sound, the anticipation of the flashing red lights kept me from sleep.

For months the Whisper Connect series held me hostage from my nightstand. Glowing in the night. Threatening me with the fear of cries and chokes and early wake-up calls. Finally, I decided it was time to take my life back the way any normal, rational woman would. I got into my car and drove over your product. Twice.

But it wouldn't break. It didn't even crack. So I tried something else.

Maybe I had a girly hammer. Or maybe it was me; maybe I was weaker than I thought. Even though I'd been awake for several hours, I still felt as though your product had just interrupted my life with hunger cries. So I visited a neighbor whose husband was a contractor and asked if I could borrow a pickax. I'm sure the fact that I was barefoot and in loungewear worried her a little. But she must have felt safe enough because she forked over the tool.

THE BEGINNING OF THE END

Which, despite my forceful attempts and good aim, didn't work. At all. So I went back and asked if she had anything else. I'm guessing she hadn't expected a second visit and wanted me as far away from her house as possible, so she handed me the real deal—a metal mallet used for smashing Sheetrock—and sent me on my way.

I'm pleased to report that the mallet finally broke your product. I guess I should have stopped smashing the monitor when the first piece of plastic flew off, but I was reliving all of the nights when I didn't sleep for more than two hours at a time. And the days when I thought she was down for a nap but wasn't. And the times she woke up too early.

In closing, thank you for creating strong, durable products that are safe for children. I'm sorry I was unable to appreciate the monitor until I dumped its remains in the trash.

Sincerely,
CK

THE BEGINNING OF THE END

I just gave birth to this much baby.

Not tonight.

BABIES"R"US

"How bad is it?" Birdy asked from behind the blue layette. I looked at my childhood friend—the girl whose heart connected with mine over bird poop—and wondered if it was safe to tell her the truth. To come clean about what it might feel like for perhaps the rest of her life. She flipped through the 0–3 shirts, holding one up every so often and tossing it into her cart. Her rosy glow was intense, and she was still pretty smiley. Maybe I'd tell her after she gave birth and it was too late. "No!" she laughed, reading my silence. "You have to tell me now. I don't want to find out when he comes near me with his *thing*. Which, did I tell you? He's already trying to do." She laughed, but I knew her well enough to wonder how she got pregnant in the first place.

The baby shifted against my chest. I looked down at her, sticking out of the carrier like a limp starfish. My cleavage was humid from the heat she radiated. My armpits and back were sweating too, because I could never do anything in moderation. Like sex. Another something I wasn't doing in moderation.

"That bad, huh?" Birdy stopped in front of the diaper receptacles and turned to me. I looked away.

"Sometimes I cry and sometimes I make mental grocery lists."

"You hate grocery shopping," she said.

I shrugged and reached for a Diaper Genie refill.

"I heard the Diaper Champ is better," she said.

"The room smells like rotting fruit either way," I said. "Save your money and use a trash can."

She pulled a Diaper Champ from the shelf and put it in her cart.

"It's like a black hole," I said. "Like there's nothing in there anymore."

"What does your doctor say?"

"Not to have sex with the baby in the room. And that 'the first few go-arounds will be less than adequate.' We actually have to keep doing it or it won't get better."

Birdy hugged me around the neck and kissed my cheek. "What does *he* say?" she whispered.

"That he's sorry. That he doesn't like it either. That he'd rather wait until my body heals. But what if it never heals? What if I never want to do it again?"

"We should get a whole year off after having kids," Birdy said. I rolled my eyes, but nodded in agreement. We reached an open register and got stuck behind a woman struggling with a stack of registry papers, a toy giraffe, and a fluorescent mobile. I dumped my refills on the conveyor belt and bounced the baby around. I caught myself bouncing nothing in the shower the other day and wondered if I'd continue the motion even after my kid could walk.

I turned back to Birdy. "You know, I leak everywhere else," I said. "Everywhere! Yet down there I'm drier than Death Valley."

Birdy paled, but as she rubbed her belly, her shoulders relaxed. For some reason that made me want to elbow her into a wall of diaper boxes. Not because I was mad at her, but because I was jealous. Jealous of the way her body worked. Jealous of how easily she laughed. Jealous that she still had the kind of pre-baby naiveté that allowed her nerves to be calmed by the simple action of rubbing her not-yet-stretched skin. "And the pain!" I added. "It's totally like I fell on the playground and scraped my vagina across the pavement."

"Is this from a registry?"

I whipped around. The cashier addressing me was cute,

well-rested, and judging by the red blotches of embarrassment on his face, probably wishing he'd taken a job next door at Chili's. My baby started to cry.

"No," I said. "Not from a registry." I bounced her faster; she cried louder.

"Phone number?" he said.

"For what?"

"F-f-for promotions and stuff."

"Oh, right," I said. "It's unlisted."

"That'll be ten fifty-eight."

I reached over my screaming body ornament and dug around the diaper bag. I grabbed my wallet. A breast pad flew out and landed on the scanner. The cashier jumped, as if all his baby store experience had taught him that disposable cotton would detonate if touched by a male hand.

Birdy snickered, muffling her mouth with both hands. But it was useless. I knew what was coming. Her uncontrollable laughter had been my companion since the night we tried to catch raindrops on our tongues and I caught bird poop instead. I hoped she peed herself. I snatched up the breast pad and shoved my credit card at the cashier. He pointed to the pin-pad machine. The baby's cry turned into a wail as I swiped the card. My ears burned, and my entire body started to sweat. Well, my entire body minus the one spot that could've used the moisture. Stupid vagina. Stupid friend. Stupid store. Stupid single guy without kids just waiting for me to leave so he could laugh at me and my stupid breast pad. Even terrible, horrible, wasteland, desert-dry sex was better than this. And I took comfort in knowing that it wouldn't be long before Birdy's heart connected with mine over that, too.

WHAT DID I DO TODAY?

Dearest, Most Involved Husband:

I'm not mad. Honestly, I'm not. There was nothing wrong with what you said. In fact, it was a fine question, and I'm glad you thought enough about how I filled my day to ask it. I'm just frustrated because I can't quantify my "activities" the way I used to. I mean, I know I did a lot of things, but they no longer equal completed tasks that I can cross off a list.

For example, if I were to catalogue my accomplishments, today's record would reflect the following:

~~Grocery Shopping~~

After reviewing my list you might get the impression that 1.) my day was a success; 2.) I had a lot of extra time to accomplish other things such as cleaning, laundry, and writing; and 3.) dinner should have been cooked and on the table. I *wanted* to do all of those things. I *planned* to do all of those things.

However, since today was grocery day, it was time to take stock of the fridge in order to make a grocery list. In doing so I found that container of breast milk I was looking for last week. Turns out I hadn't put a lid on it, so when it went sour and spilled, it seeped into the broccoli and all over the shelf, which needed to be cleaned.

Motivated by the success of a partially cleaned fridge, I yanked out the rest of the food and shelves and drawers and lined up everything on the counter. But after I emptied the contents of the door, the baby started to scream. I raced out to the porch and saw that she was on her stomach in her Pack 'n Play, which meant that I missed the first time she rolled over. And by the fiery look of hell on her face, she'll never do it again.

Upon entering the room I realized why she had screamed. She'd exploded on everything. Her clothes, her hair, and somehow even on her face. The smell was so intense that I had to coerce myself just to wipe her down and rush her up to the bath. Once cleaned, she started to yawn, so I thought I'd nurse her before her nap, since the pediatrician said I needed to "bring her to the breast" more often to combat my waning milk supply. For the second day in a row she refused to nurse long enough to create letdown. She gave a few half-hearted sucks and then thrashed her head in agony. Responding to her tears, my poor, confused body forced letdown on its own, and attempted to put out her screaming wildfire.

After depositing her in the crib, I went into our room to change. As I lifted off my shirt I found myself facing the reflection of my breasts in natural light. No wonder she didn't want to nurse. There was hardly anything left for her to latch on to. Soon my boobs would look like nothing more than raisins floating on a sea of crepe paper. But before I could sink into real tears over my loss, I heard the crib mattress shift beneath her and realized that she'd fallen asleep. I pulled on a sweater and raced down to the basement to drop off my shirt before the milk stains set. While down there I sorted through the laundry that had piled up over the week. I started a load of whites, but lost focus when I rediscovered the box of hand-me-downs from the neighbors. The good news? The baby's set on summer clothes. The bad news? You're still out of boxers.

Since I never got around to eating lunch or making a list, I wound up grocery shopping with low blood sugar and no real direction, which is why I spent so much money on chocolate cakes and salt-and-vinegar chips. And when I returned home with a fussy baby I realized that I couldn't put the groceries away since half of the fridge was still on the counter. Which is also why we're having pizza for dinner. But you need to order it. And pick it up.

So, like I said, it was a fine question. And I'm not mad at you for asking. Because I know I did things today, they just don't seem to count.

With love,

Your Wife

P.S. You might not want to go out on the porch. I just remembered that the baby's blowout has been marinating in the heat since this morning.

BAD MOMMY MOMENTS

THE (P) FILES

The Tommy-Gun Poop: In the process of sliding a clean diaper beneath the bottom of your breast-fed newborn, she shoots you with her portable, automatic firearm.

The One-Wipe Wonder Poop: After one super swipe, all is clean. You almost don't believe it, but stop yourself from questioning it further and revel in what legends are made of.

The Death-of-a-Cute-Outfit Poop: You waited until just minutes before leaving the house in hopes of avoiding this. But alas, it seeped out of the leg holes, through the tights, up the back, and into her hair. Your hair, too.

The 2 a.m. Jail Break: You haven't slept in weeks, but you knew her smell and scream indicated bottom waste. Bleary-eyed, you removed her diaper, which was when you realized that her smell and scream actually indicated gas: the precursor for what resulted in your poopy hand, the poopy changing pad, and a poopy rocking chair. It's everywhere . . . except in the diaper.

The Hide-and-Seek Poop: Where, oh where did she put her diaper?

The Wrong Kid Poop: Heaven almighty, your child is rank! Even outside in the fresh park air you can't ignore it. You lean over to get a good whiff and realize you're sniffing the butt of a child who isn't yours.

The Turdling Poop Decoy: Now it is your kid. You tackle her to the ground, grab your diaper bag, and fight through what is unquestionably the hardest diaper change to pull off. All for what turned out to be a tiny chocolate kiss. You reintroduce your daughter to park society and two minutes later you smell her again.

The IKEA Surprise Poop: Stranded in the middle of an enormous store you realize you don't have any diapers in your bag. You take your Allen wrench and concoct a toilet paper / paper towel loincloth and try to remember where you parked your car.

The Hypercolor Poop: What could she have eaten that turned her poop that many colors? And who can you tell that will care?

THE BEGINNING OF THE END

PLEASE HOLD FOR SEXY

I snuggle up behind him and trace the dream-catcher tattoo between his shoulder blades with my tongue.

"Don't do that," he says.

I roll back over. An old, battery-operated clock ticks on the wall. I stare up at the ceiling and wait for him to say something else, but all that passes between us is time.

"I'm sorry," I say. "I really want to, but . . ."

He grunts.

I know you don't believe me, but it really has nothing to do with you. You've done everything right. You've been attentive. Patient. Funny. Sweet. Thoughtful. All of the things a girl dreams her man would be. And you've been working out too, so you look hot. But somehow it just makes me feel worse about myself. Especially when you say I look sexy and I know I don't.

He rolls on his other side and faces me. I turn. We meet nose-to-nose.

We used to be so sexy together. Sneaking looks at each other in class. Racing around the city in the middle of the night. Graduating. Getting jobs. Meeting for drinks after work.

"It's okay," he says. He brushes the hair away from my face. I close my eyes and feel the tingles his fingers leave behind on my skin. "You've been amazing," he whispers. "I don't know how you're doing all of this day after day, but you are. You're a great mom." He kisses my nose.

Fifteen hours ago that would've sent me into a flurry of sexy excitement. But then today happened. Which was just like yesterday, which sucked, too.

Tears fill my eyes and I move as close to him as our bodies

allow. But I still feel nothing but the pain and soreness down there that has yet to subside. Maybe tomorrow. Maybe tomorrow it will feel better. Maybe tomorrow I'll even initiate it.

"I love you," I whisper.

"Oh yeah?" He tickles me. I laugh.

Yes. Tomorrow we'll try again. Tomorrow I'll want to do it. I'll think about it all day. I'll even drink some coffee after dinner to make sure I'm awake. *Really awake.* I'll focus on everything sexy he does. Starting now. He's pulling me close, brushing my neck with his lips. The warmth of his tongue traces around my ear. I inhale slowly, deeply. I close my eyes. I hear the intake of his breath as he whispers:

"How about a blow job?"

CRAZY LADY IN CVS: CHOOSE YOUR OWN ENDING

Chapter 117

The afternoon gets even worse. The cold rain continues. The child, still in her (stained) pajamas, won't nap, nor will she stop pulling off her socks. You are both bored and cranky. The walls slip a little closer with each hour that passes. Soon you find yourself in a box-shaped space that nestles you and the child as close as a new pair of sneakers. You need to get out of the house.

What you really need is to get out of the house *alone*, but that's not going to happen. Not today. And the only thing worse than staying in your box is the idea of preparing the child to leave it. So you don't. Instead you lie flat on your back and ignore her as she whines her way around the couch. The closer she gets to your head, the more intently you stare at the wall. You start to wonder what it would be like if you could walk on the ceiling.

Your cell phone rings. You reach out and pull your diaper bag over and dig through it without looking. You lift out your phone. Your house number flashes on the screen.

"Hello?" you say into the phone.

"Hey . . ." groans the once-masculine voice on the other end. The child climbs on your stomach and whacks you in the face with her stuffed Grover. "What's with her?" he asks.

"You couldn't just come downstairs?" you say.

"Did you pick up my prescription yet?"

"I'd be happy to . . . if I could leave her here."

Silence.

"You've been up there all day," you point out.

THE BEGINNING OF THE END

Long silence.

"I'm in a lot of pain," he says.

"It's a tooth."

"I'd really rather not be left alone with her."

You hang up the phone on your ailing husband and look over at the child, who holds the ragged Grover under her nose. Her hair is sticking up, her feet are bare, and you don't have the energy to wage the fight necessary to get her into warm clothes. Or clothes at all.

If you tell your husband to "act like a man," get his sensitive gums downstairs, and watch the child if he wants his drugs, embrace the guilt and the story is over. Good for you.

If you dump the child on his bed and leave, perhaps to pick up the prescription, but you've yet to decide, the story ends here. Again, good for you.

If your guilt gets the better of you and you decide to brave the cold weather with the child to be a Good Wife (since today is clearly not a Good Mom Day), you suck. Continue on to Chapter 118.

Chapter 118

"NOOOOOOOOOO!" she screams. You pick her up and try to put on her socks. She kicks your pelvic bone. You dump her in the crib, curl up on the couch, and wait for her to fall asleep. Thirty minutes later she's still screaming and starts to bang her head on the railing. You can hear your husband shifting in the bed upstairs, either able to sleep through the shriekstorm, or pretending really well. There is no air left in the house to breathe. You grab your keys and the screeching child and head to the car.

Some kids sleep in the car. Yours screams. You get down the street and realize that you left your money in the house. You drive back, run into the house, grab your credit card, race through the cold again, and get back into the car. You warm your hands in front of the vents for a moment and drive away. Again.

Ten minutes later you pull into the parking lot and get a spot directly in front of the door. The child has quieted down. Perhaps your luck is changing. You open her door and realize why she's stopped screaming. Her socks are off and you can't find them. It's also around this time that you realize she's not wearing a hat or a coat. It's below 40 and you forgot your child's outerwear.

You take off your coat, and try to wrap it around her chicken-bone shoulders. She screams and kicks. You worry that she's autistic. Defeated, you stuff your coat in the car, slam the door, and rush your scantily dressed baby into the CVS. A *whoosh* of warm air greets you as you slip in through the automatic doors. The baby quiets and looks around at the lights and colors. You start to breathe. Suddenly a furious bundle of polar fleece charges you. You notice the red paint on her pointer finger first, and follow it up her puffy arm to the bright foundation that might have matched her skin sometime last August.

"You should have that baby in a blanket!" she roars. Everyone in the store turns to look at you. "What kind of a mother are you? Where's her coat?"

THE BEGINNING OF THE END

If you put the child down, beat the fleece off of the crazy lady with your child's Grover, and continue on to the pharmacy, the story stops here. Congratulations. You are the woman I spent the next week wishing I was.

If you agree that you are a bad mom, shove your kid into the crazy lady's arms, and run away, go to Chapter 121, page 290.

If you tell the crazy lady off and make her cry, go to Chapter 136, page 345.

If you continue walking, pretend not to notice her (or the people staring), and pick up the prescription, you suck. You'll regret it and hear yourself changing the story a little more each time you tell it until you remember beating the fleece off of her until she cried.

i wish i still felt this excited.

MALLRATS

It was my turn to push the stroller. We didn't say anything as we switched positions, just faced forward like hikers rambling toward the top of a mountain. We wandered past the barren stores and kiosks and traded off at the base of the escalator. He didn't care that strollers weren't allowed. I did. I found comfort in following even the smallest hint of a rule. He shoved the bulging diaper bag at me. I heaved it onto my shoulder—enough diapers, toys, and snacks to take the kid camping for a week. Right here in our new outdoors.

    I looked down at the ants beneath us, streaming in through the doors and elevators. Circling the railings. All of them pushing strollers, wearing babies, or dragging little kids. We were among them now. The No-Longer-Cool who congregated in mall parking lots before the stores opened on rainy Saturdays. Grown adults so desperate for distraction that we willingly passed coffee shops we couldn't afford and stores we used to shop in, but would never enter with our kids.

    He looked down at me. We held eyes for a minute, saw through each other, and turned away. Each of us imagining a different view from the top of the mountain.

MOMMYTHING

i used to be respected at work • i used to enjoy my husband • i used to drift off on the couch when i was tired • i used to love rain on the weekends • i used to read for hours • i used to spend time by myself and taste my coffee • i used to laugh a lot, now, i'm just this mommything • mommything • mommything

RESURFACING

RESURFACING

Chips/Snacks
Growing Up/If I Wanted
A Quiet Place/I Hid
In My Parents' Garage
Soda/Bottled Water

Sugar/Flour
Cake Mixes
Now I Hide Here
Cookies/Crackers
Condiments

Canned Soup
Canned Vegeta
Canned Meats/
Gravy

THE ROAD TAKEN

Two roads diverged in a bustling store,
Where I stood against my will
Plotting my trip home to the shore,
Dreading the three-hour car-seat war
With nonstop screams so shrill.

One road was "good" and lush and straight
Or so they liked to claim.
The "bad" road would make her sedate,
But also dull and overweight,
And I would be to blame.

Although both roads would take me to
My home and those I longed to see,
I turned from "good" and all I knew,
Embraced what "bad" was sure to do,
And bought the guarantee.

I tell this as I heave a sigh
And plot our new expense,
Two roads diverged in a Best Buy, and I—
I took the one most traveled by,
And the portable DVD player with *Elmo's World* has made all the difference.

NOW I LAY ME DOWN TO SLEEP

Her whimpers persisted for an hour, often rising above the noise of the television and conversation. I trudged into the guest room she was "sleeping" in for the weekend and lifted her out of the port-a-crib. Damp from sweat and tears, she cuffed my neck and tried to hide in my hair. I carried her over to the loveseat and curled myself around her, wedging her between my body and the cushions.

Remnants of hysterics fractured her breathing. My head pounded. I was nauseated. The break of being with family turned into more stress and less sleep than I'd experienced since she was born. We were in the house I grew up in, yet I felt out of sorts and overwhelmed. She hadn't slept in the car on the way here and woke every half-hour once we'd arrived. She rejected her nap, wanting only me. No one else could feed her or hold her or play with her. Just me.

I got drowsy as we lay there. She startled herself awake a few times but relaxed as she reached for me and felt that I was there. My body warmed with hers and our breathing harmonized with the sound machine. Then she went limp in my arms and floated into the deepest sleep she'd have all night. I knew if I put her down right then, she wouldn't notice me slip back into the light of family. She wouldn't miss me.

So I stayed. Wrapped around her still body. Lulled into the night by the quieting feeling of being enough for someone.

AUTOPILOT

I sit alone at my parents' dining room table, running my nails across the vinyl covering like I once did during time-outs. It hasn't been my seat in eight years, yet this is the first trip back that feels like a visit, and not a homecoming. It's time to purge. Time to strip the attic of my adolescence so my parents can have their space back.

In the family room, my daughter scales the side of my dad's recliner, eyeing his remote control. *Good luck*, I think. Even back when it was a push-button cable box, he never shared it. As I lean back, the old lacquered chair creaks. I rock a few times and stare at the table. In front of me are three freezer bags filled with notes once passed in the halls of middle school. They are sealed with the little twist ties my mom used to pack our pretzels and cookies with. I pick up a bag and flip it a few times; the notes tumble like waves. I picture the hands that passed them to me fourteen years ago, and the faces that watched for my reaction. I sense the girls who hovered outside the classroom doors, waiting for my reply. And the anger I so carefully sealed inside the bags begins to churn.

I contemplate returning the notes to the attic. Hiding them behind the Christmas ornaments and letting them gestate for another fourteen years. Instead, I play with a twist tie until I shred the paper and expose the wire. I should throw them away, and remember them with a little wistfulness and melancholy. But that will never happen. I hoard the words of other people.

The baby cries. I look up. My mom leans her forward to give Papa a kiss good-night, but makes her release his glasses. She swings her fists in the air, nearly making contact with his nose. He smiles and blows her a kiss. He would've blown the curses of a sailor had I pulled that as a kid. My mom sings "Amazing Grace" as they pass me in the darkness of the dining room. I watch them. Invisible.

When they're gone, I open the bags and dump my old classmates on the table. Ordinary sheets of wide-ruled paper transformed into arrows, fist-sized diamonds, and rectangles, all containing my name in different handwriting. I unfold a paper arrow and mess around with it until I can refold it perfectly. And then I open it again.

Daniel's okay. My head is killing me, my tit's deformed, but I guess I'm fine. I don't know who I really like. Who do you like? —Lexie

Lexie was a wad of a girl who squeezed into the same tiny desk chair in Science each day, tormenting those of us seated close enough to see our reflections in her oily, poppy-seeded skin. Daniel was even worse, a bony instigator who grabbed my hand and rubbed his middle finger against my palm when she wasn't looking. I never had the guts to stand up to them as a kid, so it feels good to crumple them up and shove them back into the bag.

Well, are you on Britt's side? I can tell Devin is. Well, I never said to Britt that I didn't want to be friends. Just not best friends. Well, W/B! —Lori

I was excited the first time Lori passed me a note, but sober after the second and third. I only heard from her when she was rallying the troops for a fight and wanted the second-tier girls on her side to show either Britt or Devin that she didn't need their friendship. Lori's hand drifted like the sea as she wrote. I longed to imitate the loopy curvature of her letters, but her pens had the smooth ink of cartridges sold separately. Mine were erasable. All that drifted across my paper when I wrote her back was eraser debris.

I pick through the notes until I find one I don't recognize. Unlike the rest, the thin yellow paper makes me shift in my seat. I touch my misspelled name scratched in pencil.

I told you what would happen if you didn't stay away from him. Watch your back.

I can't place the girl's name or face. The boy's either. But my stomach gnaws the way it did when I realized I was alone in the locker room and there was someone waiting in the showers. My arms pulse under the memory of jagged nails cutting my skin when I was found. I still can't remember her face. Or rip her note to shreds.

Hey, look, this is not your mother speaking to you. I'm telling you as a friend. Don't mess around like that. Anyway, just out of curiosity, why did you even think about doing it? —Maria

Maria.

Maria was funny and sarcastic and a loner like I was. We said "hey" to each other and smiled when we passed in the hall. But we didn't have classes together and we ate on different lunch shifts. I remember her wrists. Bandaged with hospital tape. People mourned her as though she died. Notes flew around for everyone to sign. They awaited her return with whispers of admiration.

I turn my own wrists over, but there are no traces of my botched attempt. I spent that night in the darkness of the bathroom. Snapped one of my dad's razors. Pulled off the top blade. Thin and cold. I pressed it against my wrist and pain seared up my arm, but only a few beads of blood surfaced. I tried the other wrist. But my blood didn't flow.

It must have been the blood that got Maria sympathy, because all I got were Lexie's instructions to slice up and down the vein next time, and not across. Daniel laughed at me and grabbed my wrist, clasping it around the bandages. I sat in my corner of Science that day and held my breath, trying to pass out so I'd be excused. It was so hard to breathe.

I still can't breathe. I'm clutching the sides of the table. I know if I let go I'll bolt out the door. Run two miles to the beach and stand at the edge of the water and scream until the waves pull it all away. But the tide can't have it. It's mine.

"No!" my daughter cries. I look up. My dad is asleep in his recliner. The TV is still on, but the room is empty. "No, no, *no!*" she screams. I jump to my feet and rush toward the back of the house. I find my mom kneeling down at the doorway of my old room; my daughter backs away from her, reeling my dad's remote over her head. My mom looks up at me, bites her smile, and leaves. I sit down on my old bed. My daughter ignores me and stands on the tips of her toes to peer out the window. The same window I sneaked out of many times to find love.

I stare at her.

Long after she loses interest and wanders off, I continue to gaze as if she just climbed out the window and closed it behind her. I can't look away.

BAD MOMMY MOMENTS

CYCLICAL FORGIVENESS

I started forgiving myself a long time ago. Crying into the shower until the water went cold. Crying until the body I occupied no longer seemed my own. Sickened with remorse, I addressed my apologies like a recovering addict of bad decisions.

But even now, decades after the tears, I still don't know how to separate myself from the girl who stripped friendships for their parts. The girl who didn't want to be on the top, or the bottom. The girl who was scared of all that was lost each time she came down, but went back up again. And again. And again.

Because what if forgiveness isn't enough? What if the person I was never fades into the deep, but instead roams the waste of memories until one day she just walks back out? Passes through the life I worked so hard to hide from her, and settles into the child whose youth replaced my own. Leaving me to wonder when she'll reappear, whose face she'll have, and if she'll take what's most important to me now, just like she did then.

HER HANDS

I remember my mom's hands as petite. Cool and light and smooth. I remember their touch as though she'd just led me through traffic; or hugged understanding; or finished a prayer. And I remember the sound of the cabinet door under the sink that creaked open and signaled the kitchen was clean. Without looking, she'd reach her hand into the space between the cleaners and sponges and pull out a bottle of hand lotion. She'd lean against the counter and stare into the dark room as she removed her wedding band and squeezed some lotion into her palms. She worked it into the space between her fingers and the backs of her hands and her wrists. Always done by the time her tea finished steeping. She was somewhere else when she did this. I could slip around her and sneak a cookie and she never noticed. I always wondered where she went. Wished I could go with her.

    I spent hours forcing lotion onto my hands, trying to get them as smooth as hers. Not feeling that my skin was still naturally that soft. And then one day, barely one year into motherhood, I looked down at my hands and saw hers. The pattern of skin more pronounced. Knuckles slightly rounder, fingers calloused and dry. So I started putting bottles of lotion in the kitchen, on my dresser, in the bathroom, and in my purse: all the places I remembered her having them.

    And then one night after I finished the dishes, I opened the cabinet under the sink, pulled out a bottle of lotion, and squeezed some into the palm of my hand. I disappeared into the darkness of the room until my thoughts steeped with the raspberry tea I'd have to drown in honey before I sipped. And then I felt a tug on my leg.

    I looked down. My daughter stood there, a little shadow

against my own, and pointed from my hands to hers. I squatted down and took her chubby fingers into mine and shared my lotion with her soft, smooth skin. When I let go, she covered her nose with her hands and inhaled our matching fragrance. She smiled and wrapped herself in my arms.

Since then, her tiny face appears at the creak of the cabinet door each night, as if expecting to catch me sneaking a cookie. She watches me until I'm done and then wants to feel my hands. Wants me to hold hers in mine. Wants to disappear with me. And when I invite her in, she smiles, leans her head against my cheek, and vanishes with me into the quiet of the kitchen.

THE TOP 10 REASONS WHY I SUCK AT MOMMYING

10.) I can't do it the way I wanted to. Like with songs and sign language and learning Spanish in a bright house filled with laughter. Sometimes the closest we get to that is watching *Sesame Street* in our pajamas.

9.) I've become quiet and withdrawn. I figured that was okay since my mom was quiet and withdrawn for parts of my childhood. When I mentioned this to her she informed me it was because she was depressed.

8.) I've gained back some of the weight I lost. I blame it on the post-pregnancy cravings no one warned me about. I have two bags of chocolate going at a time. Pretzels and pita chips everywhere. Coke cans at my fingertips. And it's not because I'm lactating, since . . .

7.) My baby quit breast-feeding at six months. Breast-feeding was natural. My body provided everything for me and I *still* couldn't do it well enough to keep her interested. Since when do babies get to wean themselves? I mean, I hadn't planned to breast-feed forever, but I figured I'd get to decide when we stopped. I still miss it. Not the nursing. My profile.

6.) I look at my linea nigra more than my kid. And it's not like it's already out there to see. I have to stop what I'm doing and lift my shirt, which I do, every time I'm in front of a mirror, just in case it started to fade since the last time I checked. No wonder my child shows her belly button to anyone who looks at her.

5.) I can't make my kid happy. What am I doing wrong? She cries and whines more than any other activity, and yet most of the time I still can't figure out why. It's like I'm dating someone who doesn't even like me, but I'm so in love that I can't bring myself to break it off.

4.) I really miss my job but can't admit it out loud. I always thought being a stay-at-home mom was a one-time decision that I'd always feel good about. And yet when my friend called the other day to tell me she was looking to fill a position in her department, I immediately pictured myself in a boardroom running meetings with her. Lookin' all good with new clothes and a haircut. When my fantasy was over, I sat at my daughter's door and wept. Not only because of the guilt, but because I knew I would have to apply for the job, since . . .

3.) Running out of money isn't as simple as overspending. It was as complicated as sticking to an impossibly tight budget and scrutinizing every penny, only to find out that the budget was fine, but funds were insufficient. Yet another thing I was wrong about.

2.) I'm no longer the best at anything. Except at giving head. No lie; if it weren't adulterous and disgusting I could get us out of debt with my talent. But even my talent isn't natural. It's a result of my sex drive's year-long maternity leave.

1.) I'm not happy like the other moms around me. Why are they so happy? What do they love about being home with a kid all day? What on earth are they smiling about all the time? Why is no one else struggling? Am I really the only one out there not good at this?

PHILANDERING POTATO (II)

"You've got to be kidding me." I ripped the note off the front door just as the phone started ringing inside of the house. The baby grabbed the note from my hand. I unlocked the door, and the dog bounded over to us, barking as though we'd just broken in. I danced around her and grabbed the phone.

"Hello?" I said.

"Did you get my note?"

"Yes."

"Well?"

"Well what, Annette?"

"I thought you might be a little more concerned," she said.

"He's a cat," I replied. "They jump. Sometimes they miss. Limping is a common result."

"I'd like to take him in."

"He's fine," I said. The baby started to cry. I gave her my keys and looked away as she put the flaking grocery store tag in her mouth.

"I called all of the vets in the area and none of them had you or Harry on record," she said.

"That's because he's under my father-in-law's account and his name isn't Harry."

"Oh. What vet is he registered at?"

"He doesn't need to go to the vet for a limp, Annette."

The baby screamed at the top of her lungs.

"So you're not going to take him?"

I hung up the phone.

*

Child anchored on my hip, I searched the cabinets for something to make for dinner. Nothing. Nothing. Nothing. *Slam. Slam. Slam.* I looked in the fridge. Nothing. What did I do all day that I couldn't plan a meal? Or even just make sure there was food in the house? What kept me so busy? The dog barked as a key turned in the front door. My husband entered the house looking fresh and relaxed. I slammed the fridge shut.

"Hey, baby," he said. "How'd the interview go?"

"Fine."

"What did they say? Think you have a shot at it?"

"Maybe," I said.

The baby struggled for him as he walked into the room; he plucked her out of my arms and nuzzled her cheek.

"Hey, Poddy-Pod. You still love me, right? You're not taking a bad mood out on Daddy, are you?" She grabbed his glasses. He pulled himself back and plopped her down on the filthy linoleum. When was the last time I'd mopped? He slipped over to me and put his arms around my shoulders, resting his chin on my head.

"We'll make this work, you know. We'll split it right down the line, everything equal." He kissed the top of my head. "Please don't be mad at me," he whispered. "I really thought we could swing it on my salary."

"Stop," I said, turning to kiss him. "It's not your fault. We're lucky we realized that I needed to go back before we got into serious debt. We're even luckier that I got an interview so quickly."

"And it went well?" he asked again.

The phone rang. I turned away from him. "I'm not getting it," I said. I didn't have to look to know he was staring at me. He hated answering the phone because it was usually Grammy. It rang six, seven times. He sighed and picked up the receiver.

"Hello?" he said. "Yes. . . .Who is this?"

I turned around. He looked confused.

"Hi, Dr. Kennet. . . .Yes, Potato is our cat. . . .Oh, is she?" He closed his eyes. "A limp? Really. . . .I don't really think it's necessary. . . .Does she? No, it's not a matter of money. . . .I understand. . . .No, there's no need to put her on the phone. . . .No, it's fine. I give permission. . . .Thank you, Doctor." He stared at the phone until the operator's recording played through twice and started to beep. I handed him the note I pulled off the door. He read it, and then shoved it into the trash.

"Should we go to the vet and get the cat?" I asked.

"Let her pay the bill first. But we're getting him back. Tonight. Right after dinner." He looked around the empty kitchen. "Right after Applebee's."

FEEDING THE ONE

I hung up the phone and stared at it. Spun it around by the antenna. It slipped from my hand and clattered against the laminate countertop. I started to cry. They'd offered me more than I thought they would. A higher position, a flexible schedule, and an office with a window. I slid to the floor and buried my head in my knees. *I'm not quitting on my daughter*, I told myself. *Quitting is by choice.*

I didn't know what else to say. I had prayed so much, assuring God daily that I trusted Him to make the right decisions for our family. But His response? I'd hoped He'd sell one of my books, or prompt Grammy to give my husband his inheritance early, or maybe lay her to rest, but I knew better than to think God worked that way.

Instead I got a job offer, and a call from Sunshine Day Care saying they had room for our daughter. The old me would've been thrilled. But that was before the old me gave birth to nine pounds of guilt that now weighed twenty. So instead of calling my husband, I wandered aimlessly around the house while the baby napped. I made it to the back porch and looked around. Yet another project I'd vowed to take on after the baby was born and hadn't. It was a pit, and I knew if I didn't clean it at that moment, I'd never have time.

I rearranged toys and emptied boxes and made a mental list of what we needed for day care. Two more car seats, five crib sheets, and a slew of doubled miscellaneous items for the baby. Plus new clothes, shoes, and hair for me. Was this God's idea of help? Bleeding out our credit card? I wanted to yell, but I couldn't stop crying long enough to raise my voice. And like a good parent,

He stood back and let me get it out. He didn't interrupt. He let me clean. By the time I got to the last box my tantrum was over. I walked outside and breathed in the earthy, fall air. I was a mess. A mess employed by a company I loved. A mess who had almost everything she needed.

I got on my knees and thanked Him for seeing ahead of things. For putting the job opening into motion so that it would be waiting for us when we needed it. For taking care of my family when I couldn't see beyond myself. He filled me with peace, and I knew it would be okay, even if we had to run up the credit card one more time. I walked back into the clean porch and resolved to embrace my new life. Things hadn't changed because I was a horrible mom and secretly wished that they would. They changed because He willed them to, and He blessed every single thing I'd ever done that was in His will. He would bless this, too. I knew it.

I reached for the last box, postmarked two months after my daughter was born. It was from my cousin in Germany and had remained unopened for almost a year. I pulled everything out. Teething toys, rattles, lift-the-flap board books. My daughter had already outgrown most of the items. But the toy at the bottom of the box was perfect for her. It was an interactive piano bench. I yanked it out, and the material my cousin had used to secure it in the box fell to the floor.

Five crib sheets.

She had wrapped the piano bench in fifty dollars' worth of usable, fitted cotton. I probably would've stared at them for the next ten minutes, but the dog barked. I raced to the front of the house to quiet her before she woke the baby. And then I looked out the window and saw what she was barking at. It was my father-in-law, walking toward the house. A used convertible car seat gripped in each hand.

I opened the door for him. He set three hundred dollars' worth of plastic, cloth, and harnesses down on the living room floor. He told me that he ran into a woman at the dog park who asked if his granddaughter needed some car seats. He wasn't sure if we did, but thought he'd take them, just in case. Then he kissed the top of my head and left.

I stared down at my new items. I touched the velvet seat covers and tested the buckles. I laughed, tears blurring my view. And I thanked God again for being faithful, even though I'd forgotten that He was capable of more than I could imagine. I reached for the phone to call my husband. I was ready—really ready—for my new life to begin.

BACTERIAL FARM

I called in sick my first day back to work, incapacitated by dizziness and vomiting that ceased only when I was completely still. I forced myself to go in on my second day and wound up fleeing a co-worker's introductions to vomit into a trash can. No more "How'd you lose all of that weight so fast?" comments for me. (Though at least I was able to make it into my office first.)

Stupid day care. So glad I'm sending my little host to their petri dish. So glad other parents are able to deposit their infested kids in the toddler room without guilt or shame. So glad they're monitoring what my daughter puts in her mouth and whose runny nose gets wiped on her face. What's next? Pinkeye?

I called in sick my third day back to work with pinkeye. The upside to shelling out money we didn't yet have for day care was that I could wallow in my illness for the first time in over a year.

Me.

Alone.

In the house.

On the couch.

Watching *my* shows on TV.

Vomiting and pink-eyed, sure. But being sick in an otherwise empty house made for the best first week of work ever.

BMM/pharmacy

IF YOU HAVE ANY QUESTIONS ABOUT YOUR MEDICATION, PLEASE CONTACT YOUR PHARMACIST.

COMMON NAMES: Day Care, Home Child Care

USE: This center is used to treat children of working parents.

HOW TO USE: Place the prescribed child at assigned center between designated hours of 7am-6pm. Base the length of treatment on the individual child and familial situation. To avoid contamination, dress your child in biohazard suits complete with oxygen masks. If, after adding one degree, the temperature retrieved from under the child's armpit exceeds 102, or if he/she is dripping green mucus or expelling diarrhea, contact the childcare provider immediately and keep the child home. If the center contacts you with issues of this nature, they will require you to remove the child from the premises within the hour, and you are not to return them for 24+ hours.

SIDE EFFECTS: Guilt, sleepless nights, crying, fatigue, listlessness, trouble concentrating, loss of libido, nausea, anger, frustration, and betrayal for the attention of the teachers. FOR THE CHILD: Coughing, sneezing, yellow and/or green mucus, frequent fevers, tonsillitis, Coxsackievirus, strep throat, hitting, biting, back talk, whining, chicken pox, bronchitis, diarrhea, flu, attitude, screaming, vomiting, measles, mumps, and clinginess among others.

PRECAUTIONS: Before the initial drop-off, be prepared for screaming, crying and terrified looks of abandonment haunting you throughout your day. If you don't exit fast enough, or if you pause to look back, prepare for the sight of your child reaching for you to render your brain limp for the next hour.

MISSED DOSE: If you miss days (or weeks) due to illnesses contracted from the facilities, or for planned vacations, be prepared to pay for them anyway. Expect to take additional days off of work for field trips your child is too young to understand, special luncheons that only make them panic when you leave for a second time, and every holiday (including the ones your office doesn't observe).

IMPORTANT DISCLAIMER: The side effects listed above are not all of the possible risks that could be caused by this medication. For further information, please consult with your physician about the uses, precautions, and risks of this medication specific to your health. This information is obtained from World Data Consultants for use as an educational aid.

FOR FASTER ADMISSION, GET WAITLISTED 2 YEARS IN ADVANCE

MOMFRIEND

Dear Co-Worker:

Congratulations on the acquisition of your new MomFriend! Here are a few suggestions to help your new MomFriendship flourish.

Your New MomFriend Can (and May) Drink You Under the Table.
While she certainly is excited to be out with another adult, she downs two drinks before you finish your first because she's been trained to inhale all food-related substances when in public (as the company she usually keeps often needs to leave before the meal is over).

Your MomFriend's Spit Has the Cleaning Power of Bleach.
Do not let her use it on you. If she tries, laugh it off and make some "boundary issues" comment. She'll laugh, too. Trust me, she didn't mean to rub that mustard off your chin.

Your MomFriend Has Unheard-of Multitasking Skills.
She can carry on two live conversations without looking up. She can give the Lazy Co-Worker the evil eye, sympathize with your roommate dilemma, and teach you why you're not supposed to say things like, "Why is that man so ugly?" —all while eating soup.

Your MomFriend Can Relate Everything Going On in Your Life with Something That Happened to Her Baby.
You will be shocked to learn that the issue you're having with your boss is just like the time she taught her daughter not to leave a sippy cup of milk under the couch for a month. And those guy

troubles you're having? Just lay down the law and stay consistent with your responses. She did that last winter when her kid refused to wear clothes. Worked like a charm.

Your MomFriend Has Given Birth. This Equals Conversation Issues.
You might learn a little more about her nipples than you ever wanted to know. She will also be very blunt about things going on in your life. She has no time to nurture the conversation or soften her responses. And let's not forget—

Your MomFriend Will Cut You Off in Conversation.
It's not on purpose. She has no idea that she's doing it. She's afraid of losing her train of thought. But she's as easy to distract as her child, so feel free to cut her right back off. It'll be fun and—

Your MomFriend Will Teach You the Art of Speaking in Sound Bites.
Want to learn how to say the most, using the least number of words? Not only will it make you an asset to people with children, it will boost your annual performance review in ways you've yet to imagine.

Your MomFriend's Sweatshirt Is Absolutely Off Limits.
No matter how fashionable she is, or how cold you are, never, ever, *ever* borrow her sweatshirt. Just don't. Unless you like the feeling of stepping on a slug in the dark. Her pockets were at some point stuffed with dirty napkins or bits of unfinished food, and the sleeves were either used to apply her Clorox spit or to act as a tissue for The Child's nose.

Again, congratulations on your new relationship. We hope that you and your MomFriend will be very happy together.

Sincerely,
The Staff

LITTLE GIFTS

I still didn't know all of the language they used. Much of it I remembered from the years of meetings I'd attended. But it sounded different from this side of the table. The side with the plush chairs and extra arm room. The side that looked out into the sea of wide-eyed newbies whose expressions got a little warier the closer their seats were to us on the *other side*. Some of the more senior employees didn't care who they sat next to. But they weren't my staff. *My staff.* I had a staff. I couldn't organize my home or get my kid out of the house without running back in three times for the things I forgot, but I had a staff. A staff of ten adults in entry-level positions who were easier to manage than my one-year-old child.

As I waited for the meeting to end, I reached in my sweater pocket for a tissue and found a smooth piece of plastic. I smiled. I flipped it around in my hand and counted the sides. Six. A hexagon. I knew it was End of Summer Yellow, and its corresponding hole was right beneath the handle of the shape sorter. I hadn't put it in my pocket, but I was happy to find it there. The yellow plastic soothed me more than the first sip of caramel coffee I'd savored that morning after dropping the baby off early. I hadn't rushed because I was eager to get to work, but because my home was more of a disaster than I had the time to address, and it made me anxious to stay there any longer than I had to.

But work was different. It made sense to me. It was filled with problems I could solve and recognition for the projects I completed. The day was relaxing in its predictable busyness and downtime. Sometimes I joined adult conversations, and other times I disappeared into the personal space behind my desk. A lot of people loathed the size of the cubicles we were transplanted into after the move. They whined like teenagers about how much they missed their office doors and disliked the proximity to their neighbors. I forgave their ignorance, because they didn't have kids. They didn't understand how little space a person needs to be happy.

But no matter how good the morning was, guilt always drifted in by early afternoon. It started as little thoughts: *Where is she? What is she doing? Who's waking her up from her nap?* By four o'clock it was an unease that rumbled in my gut while I said goodbye to my staff. And as I'd close the door of my car and start the engine, it would appear in the passenger seat as full-blown dread, buckled in, and ready for the ride home.

Home.

The house, the dog, the meal I had yet to plan, the husband, the child . . . *the child.* The small person who spent her daily stipend of happiness and exploration on someone else. The baby whose mood never fit the shape of my day, no matter what form my day took. And yet even in the rush of our time together, when there were no opportunities to play and little chance of relaxed cuddling, she always gave me gifts. Items she'd slip into the pocket of my jacket when I wasn't looking. Toys she didn't play with, or utensils I didn't allow her to touch. Things that would infuriate me had I found them wedged between the cushions. But when I discovered them in my sweater during a long and mindless meeting, they were offerings of forgiveness. Because even though I felt like I was doing a disappointing job as her mom, she still loved me. She still thought of me. And even during our most trying moments, she filled my heart in a way that ten people who followed my directions and left me in peace never could.

I looked around at the faces in the boardroom; they all wore the mischievous grin I imagined on her face as she slipped the toy into my sweater. Or maybe it was a reflection of my expression, as seen by my staff, while I clutched the little secret in my pocket. The plastic hexagon of hope, yellow as the setting sun I'd see in just a few hours, on my way to pick her up.

> **What someone else said my baby did today...**

Today's snack: _Cheerios + Gold fish_

I ate: none ____   a little ____   some ____   most ____   all _✓_

Today's lunch:

I ate: none ____   a little ____   some ____   most ____   all _✓_

I drank: none ____   a little ____   some ____   most ____   all ____

I slept from : _____ to _____

Diaper changes: one a.m. _2_   one p.m. _1_

additional changes _____   rash ointment applied _____

How I felt today:

sad at drop-off _____   sleepy _✓_

happy _✓_   quiet _✓_   talkative _✓_

My favorite activity/toy/playmates: _____
exploring the class toys

Additional comments: _____
Had a great day

STANDARD OPERATING PROCEDURES

Once upon a time if I saw a child with bruises on his or her face, I assumed the child was beaten. If the parent looked frazzled, they were guilty. If they said nothing, they were guilty. If they offered unsolicited explanations for their child's colorful appearance, they were guilty. And my judgments and I lived happily ever after. The End.

Until one night—and it was a damp and chilly night—I picked up my daughter from day care and she had a black eye draped beneath her lid like a crescent moon. I asked if she fell. Did someone hit her? Did she run into something? Since she still wasn't speaking more than two words at a time, she nodded at my questions, and then screamed for the snack she knew awaited her in the car. I questioned the assistants. The lead teachers. The director. No one knew how the blackish-bluish blemish got there. And I knew as we walked out of the building without an admission in writing, the broken child was my fault.

The next morning a teacher suggested that perhaps the glaring bruise happened at home when we weren't looking, or in the car on the way to school. How dare they. *Of course it didn't happen at home.* I laughed it off, but only because I feared anything I said would make me look guilty.

Even though I wasn't.

I took comfort in the fact that her bruise would start yellowing in a few days and maybe even disappear within the week. However, I did feel compelled to inform moms at the park and anyone else who looked our way that neither my husband nor I hit our daughter. Ha. Ha. I also told everyone at work, even though most of them would only ever see her in the welt-free photos I'd tacked to my bulletin boards.

A few days later, when the bruise faded to the color of fallen leaves, my daughter ran full-force into a mortise lock with a glass doorknob. I didn't actually see the collision, but I heard the *thump/crack* combination followed by a long stretch of silence and frantic breathing. My husband retrieved her and put her on my lap before the first scream cleared our sinuses. And as she wailed, eye number two darkened. I rocked her and promised that everything would be okay. I lied, of course. Everything was going to suck.

How could I make the story sound true? Why couldn't she have fallen out of her crib, or off of the couch, or something believable? She ran into a glass doorknob? Really? And why was she taking so long to speak in sentences? She could exonerate me in four or five words if only she would string them together. And was it wrong to put foundation on a toddler? Would the natural light of the playground make it look worse? What secret steps did day cares take if they suspected child abuse? Would they question me first, or just take her away? And why, oh why couldn't someone have seen her fall the first time?

Before she even woke up the next morning, she had two black eyes. My husband kept reminding me that we didn't hit her so we had nothing to worry about. But since he wasn't the one who had to drop her off, I stopped listening. By the time I ushered her into the classroom I had completely forgotten that it wasn't my fault. I told my rehearsed truth to the teachers in a light-hearted fashion. I was calm. I was confident. They laughed at the right parts and looked concerned at the others. I was almost out the door when Miss Betty turned to my daughter and said, "Aw, sweetie, did you run into the doorknob?"

She smiled at Miss Betty and said:

"No, Mama did it."

The room went silent. We stared at her. Shocked. I don't know what I found more surprising. That she spoke her first sentence, or told her first lie. Then they all turned to me. I started to sweat. When I next revised my list of nightmares, this one might just take the top slot, edging out the reoccurring dream of my teeth getting stuck in a wad of grape gum and falling out.

"That's right, Pea." Ha. Ha. "I gave you ice for your eye."

"No," she said.

"And then I rocked you until you stopped crying, remember?"

"No!"

And then she picked her nose. Everyone groaned a little and turned back to what they were doing. I wiped her fingers with a tissue and felt myself slowly snapping out of it. It wasn't my fault. Of course it wasn't. And even though it took a full week of neurosis, accusations, and no sleep, I finally believed it. And me, my judgments, and my misleading daughter would live happily ever after. (As soon as I removed all remaining doorknobs from every building she'd ever visit for the rest of her life.)

The End.

BAD MOMMY MOMENTS

PLEASE IGNORE ME

I'M THROWING A TEMPER TANTRUM

ROUTINES, SCREAMS, AND DROPPING BOMBS

"Noooooooooo!" she screamed. Her mouth was inches from my ear. I fumbled with her car seat harness and considered having earplugs implanted. "Nooooooooo!" I gripped her to my chest and hoped she wouldn't deafen my other ear. Potato fled from the house as we entered, probably heading for the quiet of his girlfriend's place. Not that I blamed him.

"No bat, no bat!" she cried. How was I supposed to know that mentioning a bath would give her a seizure? Normally she loved baths. I loved her baths. Sometimes I even let her eat dinner in the tub because we were both so happy when she was in there.

"Naaa-ooooooo!" She flailed in my arms.

I knew I should toss her in the crib and let her cry it out, but she had streaks of dried snot on her face, grime deep in the folds around her knuckles, and mulch crumbs in her hair. Even if I stripped her down to a diaper I'd still pace outside of her door until I could wash away all traces of day care, so up to the bathroom we went.

"Nooooooooo!" She tried to run as I removed her dress, and then dropped to her knees and army-crawled toward the sink while I pulled off her diaper. And as I transferred her into the water something warm bounced off my leg. I looked down. A chunk of poop hit the floor and rolled under the radiator. It left a skid mark on my knee.

Oh, God. Was this really my life?

"No! No! No . . . no . . . no . . ." She quieted down and watched from the tub as I picked up her poop with a tissue and carried it to the toilet. It was surprisingly heavy. Excitement over,

91

she started to scream again. I wiped my leg and flushed. In the meantime she tried to escape the tub, but succeeded only in slapping her chubby arms against the porcelain. When she couldn't climb out, she yanked the shampoo and conditioner off the ledge and one of the bottles hit her in the head.

"Aaaahhhhhh! Noooooooooo!"

I grabbed a washcloth and aimed for any part of her body, but she splashed around so much that I couldn't make contact. The bath had to end, and the only way to end it would be to get a good hold on her. And the only way to get a good hold on this screaming water snake would be to get in the tub with her. I checked my watch. My husband wouldn't be home for another hour. I sighed. The water was tepid, and the color of a puddle.

Yes. This was my life.

I took off my clothes and climbed into the tub. The tragic sight of my post-child body in shallow bathwater would have amused any normal kid. Not her. She screamed when I soaped her down. Smacked the water while I rinsed her off. And raced down the hall as I struggled to cover myself with her hooded towel.

She flipped over so many times while I was securing her diaper that when I finally closed it, it was on backward and I left it like that. Lotion? She could chafe away for all I cared. Pj's? They were stuck at her wet knees.

"Nooooooooo! Not dese! Not dese!"

She threw herself against me and head-butted me in the throat. My towel dropped to the floor. Dizzy, naked, and dripping with God only knows what, I dumped her in the crib and fled the room. With the closed door finally between us, I trudged back to the bathroom, grateful that the shower would soon drown out her screams, and thankful that the Good Lord Almighty had not blessed me with twins.

DENIED

Dear Consumer:

We are very sorry to hear that you are unhappy with the purchase of Your Child. While we agree that she does in fact sound "stubborn," "maddening," "frustrating," and "out to get you," we don't believe that she is "broken." The Board discussed your lengthy petition for a replacement Child and unanimously denied your request.

Please know that we are very selective when placing a Child with a family. We take great time and effort to match personalities, talents, humor, and wills. And as one of our members pointed out, your mother sent a similar request to us concerning you twenty-seven years ago; we denied her as well.

We suggest that you keep up your level of creativity. For instance, we studied the "I Want a New Mommy!" incident and were quite impressed with your calm, proactive response. Bundling her up and hiking her over to the mall to help her shop for a new mommy was just what she needed to snap her out of her funk. We especially liked the nice touch of telling her how much you'd miss her if she left *after* she changed her mind and apologized. Well done.

We also approve of the "No Warning" system you installed in her life. You go over the rules on a regular basis and when she breaks one, she faces immediate consequences. This makes sense to her, and while she doesn't like it, she respects you more when you stick to your system.

However, the Board feels that you still have some serious work to do. On yourself. We are happy with your progress over the last few years, but your pride and laziness continue to cause flare-ups. Stop comparing her to other people's kids and yourself to other mothers. Stop worrying about their opinions on your parenting style. Frankly, if you weren't so judgmental, you wouldn't think so many people were judging you. We also suggest that you work on your will. It has softened a little over the years and needs sharpening if you hope to stand a chance when Your Child turns twelve.

The more we examine the placement of Your Child, the more we applaud our initial decision to join the two of you together.

Carry on,
Consumer Affairs, Heaven

MONDAY

21

i used to feel guilty for going back to work.
now i feel guilty for looking forward to Mondays.

BAD MOMMY MOMENTS

date _____

Dear Diary,

I totally got busted rockin' out in my car.

You know I can't help it. You know how I get after I drop her off at school. And you know if it's above 50° I have the windows down.

It was 58°.

Diary, I'm so embarrassed.

I stopped at a red light but was so into my song that I didn't notice the 2 guys in the car next to me.

And then I looked over and they were smiling at me. They said something but I couldn't hear them over my music.

And then they laughed.

They laughed at me, Diary.

And then the next song came on.

And I realized I'd been singing,
"PUT DOWN THE DUCKIE"

Diary, I don't know if I can go on.

Luv,
me

P.S. You'd better not tell my mom I said that.

BANK ROBBERIES AND SUNSHINE

"Go! Go! Go!" I bang my hands against the steering wheel. The cars ahead of me don't budge. The light taunts yellow. Then red. Again. Why? I push the door open and hoist myself up on the frame, and then the seat. Other drivers do the same.

Cruisers obstruct the intersection, blocking traffic all four ways. A Tercel thwarts them and turns the corner. The driver leans out of his window, says something, and moves to the next car. One by one, the vehicles ahead of me U-turn and dart off in the opposite direction. Finally, the Tercel pulls up parallel to me. "There was a bank robbery up there," he says. "Guy got away on foot."

A bank. A bank. Where is there a bank? I search the buildings until I find the bank . . . directly across the street from the church. The church my daughter's day care is in. My peripheral vision darkens. I start to hyperventilate. *Focus.* I slide back into my car and U-turn into oncoming traffic. Floor it to the next light. Squeeze across the stopped vehicles and onto a back road. Where am I?

Officers block the through streets and force the traffic forward with arms and whistles. No one can park. I ditch my car in someone's driveway and slam the door behind me. K-9s and cops with shotguns advance in my direction.

"Ma'am! Get back in your car and don't move!"

"But my . . ."

"Ma'am!"

I wait for them to pass and take off again. I barely feel the pain as my heels smack five minutes of uneven pavement.

Almost there.

Three more streets.

Two.

One.

Blue-and-red lights cluster the front of Sunshine Day Care. Yellow crime tape blocks the sidewalks and bus stops. Cops redirect traffic.

"Lady, turn around!"

"I need to get into this building," I say.

"Now!"

"My daughter's in there! Please!" I edge forward. The cop stares at me.

"Don't come back out," he says.

I tear through the parking lot and throw myself at the door. Door code. Door code. What is the . . . 4326? 4362? 4236. *Click.*

I yank the main door.

Push double doors.

Run past the office.

The Fun Room.

The baby room.

I stop at the toddler room. A thick smell of lunch and diapers hits me as I enter the dark space. The soft piano of a Mozart lullaby draws me in. I scan the floor. The toddlers are all on their cots, babbling or sleeping. My hands tremble as I close the door behind me. I sit down next to her bed. She rolls over.

"Mama!" She climbs out of her blankets and burrows into my arms. "Mama." She wriggles away to show me her shoes and where she left Grover. She sits back down and pushes away a friend who gets too close to me.

I breathe in her hair. My muscles relax.

I rock her.

I breathe her.

I hum in her ears.

"Mama's here, Pea."

I keep humming in her ears, breathing and rocking. *Mama's here.*

MAMA'S (STILL) HERE

Why are you calling me again? What could've possibly changed since we met here two hours ago, an hour before that, and forty minutes after you first fell asleep? Didn't we glide into the evening with billowing sheers and Vivaldi's guitars? Didn't I smother you with stories and kisses and affirmations? Didn't the neighborhood—and your father—set the example of how to fall asleep and stay asleep? Aren't you tired?

Why are you smiling at me? You know I can't smile back. Even if it wasn't a matter of principle, I can't open my eyes wide enough to make it to your crib without tripping over the toys you threw on the floor. You shouldn't be playing this late. Why do you refuse to acknowledge the night? Have you forgotten that you've left the womb and it's no longer acceptable to kick me while I'm trying to rest? Is it because while you slept in my uterus I scoffed that I'd never work just to pay someone else to raise you, and tonight I took credit for how much better you're turning out now that someone else is? Is it because I still haven't figured out how to be with you on the weekends while I'm recovering from work and trying to complete in forty-eight hours what I put off for five days?

Why must your cries erode what little rest I get? Is it because sleep is one more thing that separates us? Is it because it's the only time I'm here when you call? Is it because I once didn't feel as though I existed as a person, and am now so busy existing as multiple people that I don't have time to respond unless you're loud enough to force my body from REM like a carbon monoxide alarm?

And why do you only want me? What about Daddy? Even with work and everything else I'm doing, *he still sees less of you than I do*. He should experience your shallow sighs and the smell of yellow shampoo in the moonlight. He shouldn't miss out, all alone in that big, warm bed with piles of covers hugging his body instead of your little arms and the stiff glider cushions. You should rouse him from calmness and slumber so he can ponder these things in the middle of the night instead of feeling so well rested that he gets those "we-should-have-another-baby" eyes.

 You're wide-awake. Can't you see what's happening? He's got the baby itch again. His clock is ticking. And it never runs down because his alarm doesn't go off in the middle of the night. You think you don't see much of me now? Forget it. If he knocks me up again, you'll get less of me during the day and none of me at night, because I'll be with the baby. And who will you be with? Him. So why don't you do us both a favor and start calling for him now? He's bigger and warmer and so much more comfortable to snuggle with than I am. And you'll love being in his arms so much that you'll never want to share him with a sibling. And you won't have to. Because after a week or two of broken sleep, he'll never ask me for another baby again.

 So please just call for him.

 Please?

BUDDIES, 2007
PHOTOGRAPH BY C.Zona

We love to make Daddy laugh.

To do this I embellish stories, get him drunk and take him to comedy clubs.

You, on the other hand...

The other day he farted and cracked himself up. You turned to him and said, "My try!" and ripped one across the room. It was the first time I saw him laugh so hard he had to sit down.

Since I don't fart, you win.

INSTEAD

Loving him hadn't been part of the plan. Most of the time I couldn't stand him. He wrote on the fly what took me hours to edit, and had the kind of public ease I coveted in others. But he was funny, and thoughtful, and had a way with sarcasm that drew me in like nicotine, blowing out my forgotten words in perfect circles of white smoke around my head. I wanted him to find me interesting, even though I wasn't interested in him. I wanted him to want me.

Instead, I wrote him a "you're not The One" e-mail, because I didn't have enough eye contact to say it in person. He disagreed, but stuck around to be my friend anyway. Every once in a while he'd invite me to get coffee, or go to the zoo, and I'd remind him that losers liked caffeine and the only animals belonging in the city were either on leashes or pelted into the street. But since he never gave up, I was never anything but satisfied.

And then I walked into film class one afternoon and found him sitting in the middle of the theater with a girl I didn't recognize. Her brown hair was the shade of his, and cut in layers that swayed when she laughed at his jokes. They had matching foil-wrapped cheesesteaks dripping with cart juice, and I could tell by the way she handed him napkins that they'd had cheesesteaks before.

The movie was loud and the room was too dark to read their lips, so I stared. I stared at the smooth symmetry of his profile when he smiled, and the definition of his arms when he stretched. I didn't have to look down at his hands to know they were just the right size to hold both of mine in one of his. But it didn't matter, because she probably drank coffee and liked animals.

He kept coming around, though. Lingering at my dorm long after classes ended, pulling out cards, and challenging me to rummy. We played a lot of rummy. And he always sat just far enough away that I noticed the distance. Our hands never accidentally bumped while plucking cards. Our knees never touched. His eyes were on me when I looked up, but he allowed me the space I'd told him I wanted, even though what I really wanted was to close my eyes and feel his lips draw out the breath I lost when he passed by me, walking with her. Instead he'd shuffle, I'd cut, and he'd deal a game that would last too long, letting me win by default. And for the first time in my perfectionistic, Type A life, I didn't care about winning, even at a game I'd made up.

I was Super Happy Waitress at the diner back home over winter break, counting down the days until he promised to visit. I felt sexy in my maroon polyester ensemble and even put on eyeliner, just in case he could see me from three states away. According to my tips, I'd never been so charming, pleasant, and fast. Ironic. I'd also never served so many wrong omelets, or left so many people without refills, in my career as a food pusher. A counter regular heckled me from behind her bread pudding one night, announcing that I was in love. She meant this as a put-down, because she wanted everyone to know that I'd forgotten to sprinkle extra cinnamon on her dessert. I doused her soggy custard with enough spice to leave her sneezing and slipped into the kitchen to ponder her remark.

I continued to ponder as I waited for the DC train to arrive. I was an hour early; Amtrak was not. I imagined how he'd look, walking toward my car. Head down, facing away from the icy rain. Wide shoulders hunched. I wanted to fling open the door at the sight of him, jump into his arms, and squeeze my legs around his waist. Instead, I turned off the heat and let the outside air cool me down so that he wouldn't see how flushed I was.

That night he slept in my bed. I was situated across the house on a pull-out couch that *wasn't* my bed. I waited until I was sure everyone was asleep and then panicked. The house had been quiet for an hour. Why hadn't he come out to where I was? What if the tension was only mine? What if he was peacefully sleeping in there, content with being my friend? I wanted to hide under the quilt until the sun forced my awkwardness aside for another day. Instead, I slipped through the dining room, the kitchen, the living room, and the hallway until I was right in front of my bedroom door. I stood there for a few minutes, hand on the knob, shaking with adrenaline. Never had I been so excited to enter my room.

I opened the door. He was sitting up, a shadow in the cone of moonlight filtering in through the window. I stepped onto the soft, quiet carpet. He reached out his hand. I was right. Both of mine fit in one of his. He pulled me in, just the way I'd wanted him to since the day I'd watched him in film class. We looked at each other. He touched my cheeks, slipping his fingers toward my chin. I closed my eyes, trembling as his thumbs brushed over my lips, parting them by his touch. I felt his hands move behind my neck and through my hair, gently guiding my face to his. And when his lips finally reached mine, softness and warmth spread through me, and I knew it was okay that I loved him.

Six years later, as he reached to take our daughter from the nurse, I watched him again. His broad shoulders hunched. His eyes focused. His body concentrated on sitting down without dropping her. And instead of looking up for help, he tucked her against his chest, lifted the stocking hat above her eyes, and sang:

> *Oh, I've seen fire and I've seen rain*
> *I've seen sunny days that I thought would never end . . .*

He overwhelmed me with the softness of his voice, and with who he was, and with his desire to be mine. And even though I had loved him again and again over the years, I knew as I watched him with our baby that I must not have *really* loved him until that moment.

"The one that looks like a candy cane,"

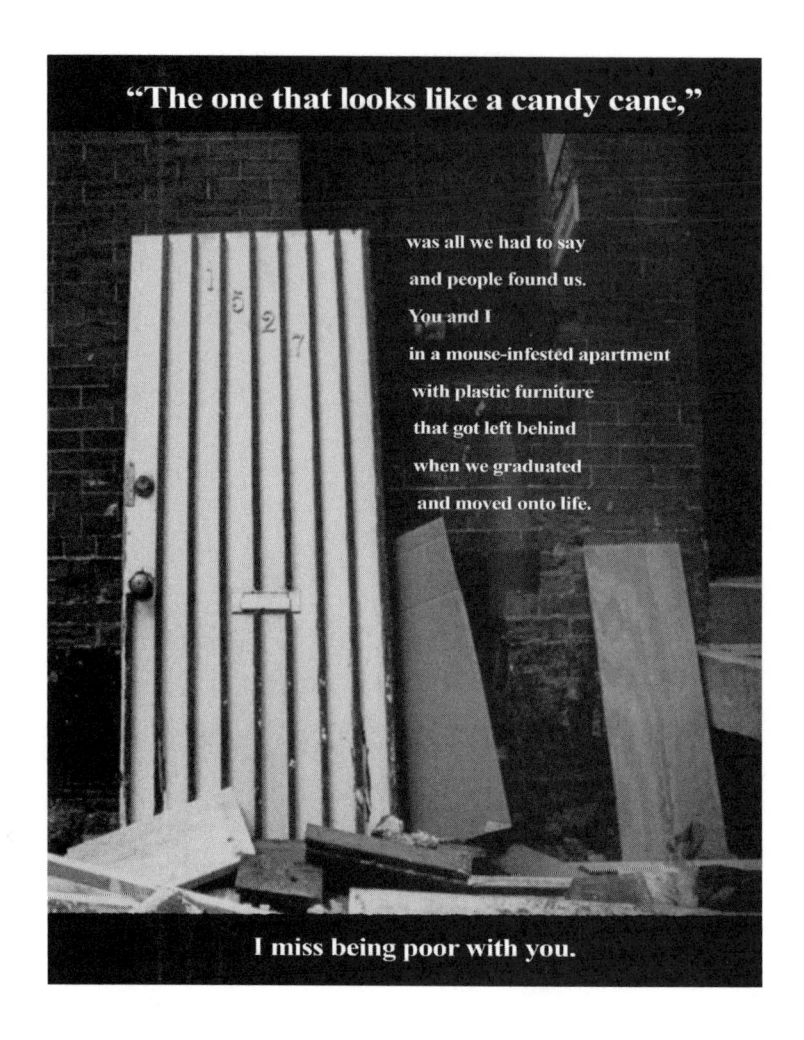

was all we had to say
and people found us.
You and I
in a mouse-infested apartment
with plastic furniture
that got left behind
when we graduated
and moved onto life.

I miss being poor with you.

WORDS

I never wanted us to be that couple who went to breakfast and read the newspaper. Quiet. No eye contact. Synchronized smiles, but not at each other. They always seemed at peace in their silence; I guess they were fine with running out of things to say. But we fell in love over words. The sound of our keyboards beating with breath. And I feared if we ran out of words we'd have nothing.

And I never thought that someone made from us would use all of the good words, leaving everything else to sound the same. But she did. I know it's not her fault and life just happened that way.

But sometimes . . .

When I really miss them . . .

You . . .

When I really miss you . . .

I read through our old words, searching for traces of the kids who teased, and laughed, and brainstormed late into the night, but I can't find us anymore. Were we ever there? And I can't bring myself to look at you over my sadness.

So instead I look away.

Breathe.

Smile about something else.

And reach for the newspaper.

HOME

"Hey, Boo!" he called from downstairs.

"I know, I know!" I shouted. "I'm almost done!" I checked the clock and rummaged through my makeup bag. If I left in five minutes, I'd still make it to work on time. I fumbled with the mascara.

"No! No! No!" he yelled. The baby screamed. I jumped, causing the inky wand to darken and enhance my eyeball. I raced into the hall, rubbing my eye. He met me at the top of the stairs, dangling our child over the baby gate. She cried louder when she saw me and struggled out of his arms. I reached for her and she grabbed my neck, snuggling into my chest.

"Are you okay?" I looked at her. She was pale and a little cross, but she was always pale and a little cross. I turned to my husband. "I don't get it. What just happened?" In response, she spewed on my face. My husband gagged and rushed back downstairs to the bathroom.

I stood there. Stunned. I hadn't been sideswiped by the Puke Truck since we transitioned into sippy cups.

"Mama clown?"

Sour milk and cereal frizzed patches of my flat-ironed hair. My shirt was stained. My face was now a canvas of unnatural colors. *Yes. I am a clown. A sad, sad clown.* I put her on the floor and wiped my nose on my sleeve. She tugged on my leg. Her eyes were glassy and her cheeks were red. No wonder she was pale and cross.

"C'mere, Pea."

"No!"

"I just want to see if you're hot."

"No!" She raced into her room and slammed the door,

popping the lock in and out. I turned the knob. It wouldn't budge. I turned it again, harder this time, and rattled it. She giggled, but wouldn't let me in. It was locked.

I checked my watch. I was late. But if I left in ten minutes, I could still make it to the studio by the start of rehearsal. I washed my face and flipped through the shirts I'd decided against that morning. The downstairs toilet flushed. Heavy tread took the steps two at a time.

"She can't go in today, you know that, right?" I called.

Silence.

Oh, no, I thought. *Uh-uh*. I inspected my sticky hair in the mirror so I could evaluate his expression as he entered the room. He sat on the bed, rested his head in his hands, and exhaled. *No. No way*. It was *his* turn. No way was he pulling this again. I changed before he could open his mouth and hurried past him toward the door.

"I have a client flying in from California for the big meeting I'm heading up this morning and . . ." he said. He looked up.

"No," I said. "I stayed home the last two times. I can't miss another teleconference—I'm supposed to direct it!" I could feel my face flushing. This was not happening again.

"But there's someone to cover for you," he said. "You have a backup. I don't."

I looked at him. There was no vomit anywhere on his person.

"I thought you said she threw up downstairs," I said.

"Oh, she did."

"Where?"

"The couch," he coughed, "and in the toy box."

I slammed the closet door. *Of course I had a backup*. I stomped over to the dresser, yanked open a drawer, and pulled out a T-shirt. "Well, you'd better start cleaning up if you want to make it to your meeting." I marched into the bathroom and locked myself in.

"Everything equal." Right. Sure. Equal as in we both drive to work. Equal as in we both come home at the end of the day. But I was the one who did the day care runs. I was the one who missed work for those stupid lunches and field trips. I was the one who cooked dinner and cleaned the kitchen. I was the one who ran errands on the weekends.

I yanked the straight iron from the outlet and dumped the hot equipment under the sink. Swept all of my makeup into a drawer and slammed it. My compact fell to the floor, shattering the little mirror.

"You okay in there?" he asked.

"Where's the baby?" I said.

"In her crib."

"Why is she in bed already?"

"I put her in there while I cleaned up. She fell asleep."

Oh, sure, she goes right down for him. Now she'll never take a nap. I opened the door and pushed past him. He grabbed my arm.

"I don't think my job is more important than yours," he said.

"Right."

"I just can't miss this one particular meeting." His voice softened. "I can miss the rest of my meetings, though, so I'll be home around eleven and we can switch off. You'll be there in time for the shoot."

My shoulders slumped as I calculated the time. He was right. I would make it. I still couldn't look at him, though.

"I just have to be there for this meeting, okay?"

I nodded. He opened his arms. I leaned against his chest.

"Wait!" He pushed me away, but it was too late. I had vomit on my face again. "I forgot. She got sick on my shirt before

I put her down."

*

She and I sat together on the couch and watched *Elmo*. She was snuggled against my leg, clutching her Grover. I rubbed her head with one hand and scrolled through e-mails on my laptop with the other. She drifted off to sleep as Elmo asked a baby how he walked a dog. When her fingers fell from her lips, I stopped rubbing her head so I could type with both hands. I moved as lightly as I could, but she woke up anyway, grabbed my hand, and put it back on her head. I smiled and resumed the head stroke.

"My mama," she sighed. Her eyes closed as she nestled into my leg. "Mine."

I stared down at her expression, determined even in sleep. I stared at the thin, wispy remains of her disappearing mullet, and at her profile that was thinning out. I stared at the outline of her body that was at least two-and-a-half times bigger than when the nurses first handed her to me. I ditched the laptop and stretched across the cushions, drawing her up on my chest like a blanket. I watched her until she wedged herself into the nook of my arm with the jerky movements of a newborn. How could I have wanted to drop her off at day care like this? How could I have hoped to play it off so they wouldn't notice she was sick? How could I have been so angry about leaving work early to attend functions with this little person who still needed me? Still wanted me?

I felt around on the floor for my cell phone and dialed his number.

"I'm outta here in five minutes, I swear," he answered.

"No, no," I said. "I just, I mean, don't worry about coming home early. I'm good to stay home."

"You sure?" he said.

I gazed down at my messy blonde baby.

"Yeah. I'm sure."

THE
END OF THE BEGINNING

THE NEW NORM

PHILANDERING POTATO (III)

The weather finally broke. The ground was mushy. The air, while not warm, relented just enough that we could inhale and not get dizzy. My daughter and I took Maggie for a walk; her walks had been reduced to circling the park three times, but at the speed of a toddler, she was assured at least twenty minutes to roam unencumbered. About a quarter of the way into our first lap, an orange flash darted out from behind a bush.

"Look who it is, Pea!" I smiled; we hadn't seen him in almost a week.

The baby dropped my hand and shuffled over to Potato. He backed up as she advanced, his tail tocking like a Felix the Cat clock. He waited until she reached for him and then slinked over to me.

"Titty!" she said.

"That's right, it's the kitty!"

Potato rubbed against my legs, permitting me to stroke his fur. His soft, silky, freshly groomed fur. It was like he wanted me to know that he had just had his body handled by someone who wasn't me.

"Titty, Titty, Titty," my daughter sang.

We resumed our journey and the cat followed from a distance. People always got a kick out of watching us walk. Dog in the front, family in the middle, cat in the rear, like a second dog. Except dogs are loyal.

*

At first I thought e-mail would be the best way to communicate with her. It was passive aggressive and I knew it, but I enjoyed making her wait for my response. Seeing her name in my inbox infuriated me, though. She was everywhere. Stealing my cat. Stealing my thoughts. Stealing space on my hard drive with her guilt because she couldn't figure out how to tell him that even though she was leaving on vacation, she would always come back for him.

"It's like getting one of those ridiculous family update letters at Christmas," I said and closed out of my e-mail. "Except that it's not Christmas and she's not family."

"Well, what did you think would happen if you agreed to 'share' the cat?" my husband said.

"I didn't expect to work as her personal assistant."

"You can't share a cat," he said.

"Oh! Did I tell you what she said the other day?"

"The baby?"

"No, Annette. She actually said they'd be happy to take the cat 'off of our hands' if we thought about giving him to a shelter or putting him down because we're 'too busy with the baby.' I mean, come on! He's a cat."

"Yeah," he said.

"Hello?"

"What?"

"Are you listening?"

"Yeah. I heard you the other two times you told me this story."

"Did you care either of those times?"

"I already told you what I thought we should do," he said.

"Oh, what? Ransom the cat for ten thousand dollars? Great idea."

"Look," he said. "They spent how much on chemo for their last cat? And it died. This one is alive, so it's got to be worth more. Besides, what they're doing is so messed up. The least they could do is pay us for the cat they've stolen."

"I'm not selling the cat," I said.

"And I'm not talking about it anymore."

*

A urinary tract infection, she wrote in her e-mail. A feline UTI. Of course Annette was the one who figured out something was wrong with him. She was the one who could work from home and watch him all day. She was the one who got the go-ahead to put him on official house arrest, as opposed to the unofficial house arrest she'd sanctioned over the last year. Thank goodness she sent a series of friendly e-mails informing me that I could visit my own cat at her house whenever I wanted, otherwise I might have been bitter.

Plus, I wasn't sleeping well due to my daughter's multiple-nightmare nights. Plus, work took up more time than I'd expected, and the money didn't stretch as far as I'd hoped. Plus, my husband and I fought each time we received an e-mail from Annette. Or saw her. Or realized how long it had been since Potato last visited.

I turned away from the computer. I was exhausted from dodging Annette's confrontations, my husband's confrontations, and the confrontations I knew were waiting behind a dark corner in my mind. I knew I'd promised to share the cat, but I had a small child. Surely that came with the same warnings as narcotics: you should not operate heavy machinery or make any decisions about traitorous family members while consuming new motherhood.

I just missed my cat. So I marched over to Annette's house and banged on her door. Her eyes widened as she took me in.

"It was a good thing I was home with the cat today," she twittered. "Or I might not have noticed . . ."

"Give me the cat. You can't keep him."

"It's just for two weeks," she said.

"No, it's not," I said. Potato jumped down off of his kitty perch and rushed over. I looked around their living room. A cat post and toys that matched her décor were placed along the parameters of the room. Like a nursery.

"Can he at least come here while you're at work? I've arranged to work from home until he's better," she said. Potato stood between us and arched his back. I snatched him up.

"He's a cat, Annette. *My* cat. My husband's cat. My daughter's cat."

"But what if he gets sick when he's outside?"

"We're keeping him inside now. He'll be fine. We'll be by tomorrow with a check to reimburse your investment at our vet's office." I turned and marched Potato back home. He leapt out of my arms as we walked through the door. He inspected the rooms. Slept on our bed. Woke us in the morning for his breakfast. It was like he'd never left.

I called the vet as soon as I settled into my cube at work the next day. I explained the situation and asked that they strip Annette from the account. The receptionist understood. She said it happened often between neighbors and outdoor cats. She also informed me that Potato's test results were in, since I'd forgotten to ask about them. His UTI was worse than they'd thought. If he hadn't come in when he did, he might have died. I thanked her and hung up.

I couldn't focus. Every time I tried to start a project or an e-mail, rage built up inside of me until I left my desk and paced. My day was a jumble of elevator trips, hall wanderings, and staring. I stared at the ceiling. I stared at my monitor. I stared at the photographs that marked my daughter's progression from a blob to an independent child. By afternoon I started to relax. Potato was home. It would be okay. My phone rang.

"Hello?" I said.

"It's Annette. I just called the vet for the results of Harry's tests and they told me they could no longer share any information about him."

I leaned my head into my hands. "He's not your cat," I said.

"I know, but I just want to make sure he's okay."

"He's fine."

"Could I come by and see him?"

"Annette..."

"I know, I know. Some of my friends are telling me that I've taken this too far, but please..."

"Good-bye," I said. I hung up the phone and wandered back over to the elevator bay. There was nowhere to go, but I couldn't sit at my cube. The elevator doors opened. I got in and pressed the down arrow. I leaned my head against the mirrored wall. *Oh my God*, I moaned. I didn't mean that as a petition for God's help on the issue. In fact, I'd gone out of my way to exclude Him from what was going on. Not like He could argue the principle of the matter, it was solidly in my favor. But my mumblings must have qualified as a prayer, because a cool sense of peace washed over me. I reached for it. I wanted to keep it. But I knew the peace would come at a price. It always did.

I struggled with the new idea the whole way home. What was it worth? What was more important? And even if I wanted to do it, how could I get my husband to agree after everything that had happened? After everything we'd said. I pulled up at the house and made it to the front door before realizing that I'd forgotten to pick up my daughter from day care.

*

I stroked Potato's soft fur. The vibration of his purring eased through my fingers as I waited for my husband to return home. The cat closed his golden eyes and rested his chin in the crook of my elbow. He looked as though he were smiling. He probably was, little rat. He *would* smile at this. I closed my eyes and listened to my daughter boss her grandfather around on the porch. She was so lucky to be two. Nothing sucked this bad when you'd only been alive for seven hundred and thirty days.

"Tell me you're kidding," my husband said as he pushed through the front door. I jumped to my feet, dumping Potato on the carpet; he shook me off and streaked across the room. My husband scooped him up. I stopped them before they could enter the living room. If they sat down, it would never happen.

"Fine," my husband said. "But you're gonna have to do it alone. You know how I feel about your public scenes."

"Please?" I whispered. "She'll never stop unless we do this together. She needs to see that we're in agreement. Because we need to be okay about this. Are we?"

He rubbed Potato's head; his purrs raged like the kitty Harley he probably had parked in front of his kitty condo at his kitty girlfriend's house. "You're a whore, Potato. You know that?" He looked at me. "Let's get this over with."

Annette opened the door before I finished knocking. When she finally made eye contact with me, she took a step back. Her mouth fell into a gaping O.

"We haven't changed our minds about sharing the cat," I said. "It's not fair to us and it's not fair to our daughter. But we know how much you love him. You saved his life. So we want you to have him." My husband handed her "Mr. Fluffy." I gave her his medical records.

"This is not what I . . ." Her husband appeared and they nuzzled the cat. "Thank you," they said. They cooed at him, whispering things we couldn't hear. Unreal. We never could have competed with that. And now we didn't have to. My husband put his arm around me and pulled me close as we walked back to our house. He kissed the top of my head. The peace I'd sensed in the elevator washed over us, and for the first time in weeks, I felt great.

YOU/HIM

YOU: I'm not looking at them, okay? It's still naptime. *My time.*

HIM: I don't even remember this stage anymore. Almost feels like it never happened.

YOU: Well, it did. And now it's over. Enough with the photos.

HIM: I can't even recall the basic things. Like size, or weight, or how quickly it all changed.

YOU: You need to put the pictures away.

HIM: I just wish I'd spent more time taking it all in. Appreciating it.

YOU: Appreciating what?

HIM: I want another chance.

YOU: Another chance with what? Her? Go get her. She's awake. You can try again all afternoon.

HIM: No, not with her. Another baby.

YOU: *What?*

HIM: It's just that . . .

YOU: Wait. Are you looking at a picture of my nursing tits?

Silence.

YOU: Seriously? I can't believe that you'd . . . hold on, let me see that one. Wow, they were *huge*.

Silence.

YOU: No, no, no. Forget it. I'm not falling for this. No more kids. We're done.

THE END OF THE BEGINNING

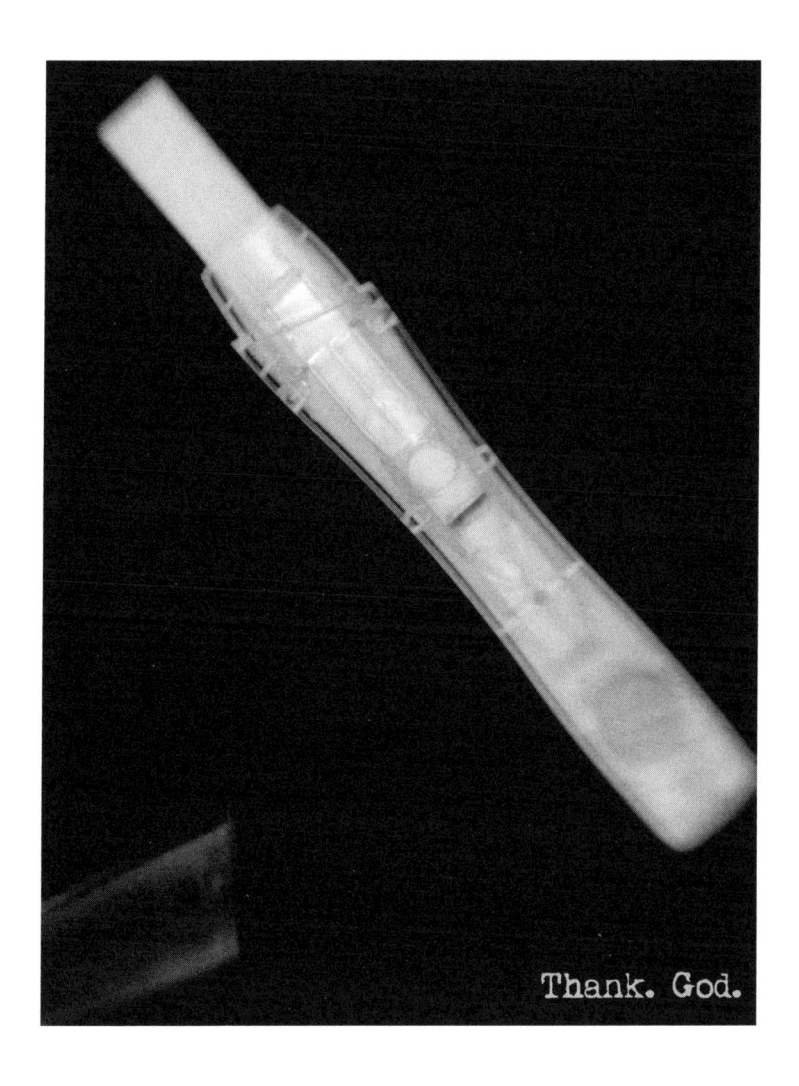

LADYBUG RAIN BOOTS

The phone call came while we were getting ready to play in the rain. We'd been expecting it for three years but never thought it would come. We saw you two nights before, resentful that we had to lug a toddler to a nursing home along with the wicker basket and beach towel you'd requested that week.

We often enjoyed our visits when you permitted us to come alone. When you were pleasant and we could speak with you instead of worrying about whose open room the baby would run into, or what heirloom she'd get her hands on before we reached her, or how much time we had before she got bored and started to whine. But you wouldn't see us without her anymore.

Lately, you barely noticed when we were there. You'd open your eyes just long enough to tell her you loved her and hand her the box of cereal you saved from your breakfast and make sure that she still knew who you were. Then you'd apologize and close your eyes again. In those moments I forgot how difficult you could be. Instead, I thought of the times I sat with you and fed you your vegetables, wiped your chin after you drank your milk, or encouraged you to try again with your walker. And I thought of the way you proudly waved to your caregivers, the same pride my toddler had for her own gestures.

When I think of you now I remember the pleasure you took in sipping your cappuccino and calling into the room everyone who passed by, introducing them to your great-granddaughter again. You died before she could tell you she loved you. But she recognized the building you lived in and she'd point and call your name as we parked, anxious to rush inside and give you her Grover. She still asks for you, and recognizes your face in photographs. She even sees you in her picture books.

I think of you a lot. I look around my life and know that much of it is because of you. And I wish that our last visit had been one of the times we laughed and said we loved each other, instead of me sneaking out of the room when I realized you were medicated for the night and didn't know we were there. As we drove away I knew I'd never see you again, but I didn't turn back. I didn't want to. I'd felt it many times before. And maybe I was wrong again.

It was easy to be wrong about you.

Then the call came, early on New Year's Day. I sat on the stairs and watched your great-granddaughter as she tugged on her raincoat and looked for her ladybug rain boots. I pictured the puddles she'd splash in and how the winter rain would feel on my face, dissolving the tears and the chance she'd notice something was wrong. I decided against a coat for myself and ushered her outside, needing to feel the cold, and grateful for the rain.

HIM/YOU

HIM: She's getting so big. You don't miss the little baby?

YOU: She's still pretty small.

HIM: And she's not waking up at night as much.

YOU: Oh, no?

HIM: And it's not like we'd have two of them in diapers at the same time.

YOU: Right.

HIM: And you lost all that weight so quickly.

YOU: Well, that's true.

HIM: All the moms I work with were totally jealous.

YOU: Really?

HIM: And it would be pretty cool to get your tits back.

Silence.

HIM: For you, I mean.

YOU: Because . . .

HIM: Well, it's not like I can touch them without getting all wet. From the milk, I mean.

Silence.

YOU: So we're done here?

HIM: Yep. One it is.

FEETIES

She stood at a crosswalk fifty feet from my car. Her back was straight and stiff, mummified by a crisscross of material tied in a knot at the base of her spine. I could feel the restraint of her carrier across my chest, and the lump of a newborn pulling down on my shoulders. She gripped a small hand in each of hers and didn't budge as the two attached kids tried pulling her into traffic; she was a well-rooted tree on the corner of 50th and Mason. I took a deep breath on her behalf. Three kids under the age of five. I wondered what expression she wore. Exhausted? Angry? Vacant? It was rush hour on a cold morning and the four of them were already dressed and out of the house. She had to be near tears.

    I glanced at her face as I drove by. She was smiling. A real smile, too. The kind that included teeth and laughter and had eluded me for so long that I couldn't keep myself from smiling in response. And that was when I saw them in my rearview mirror: the teeny little feeties sticking out of the sling. My stomach twisted at the memory of my daughter's feeties. How smooth they felt on my cheeks as I changed her diaper, or tried to get her to smile. Her wrinkled, nubby feeties.

    I pictured two boxes in the corner of the attic, the plastic one that contained newborn clothes, and the cardboard one with the baby carrier inside. My daughter hated that thing. She twisted and writhed until I gave up and lifted her out. Maybe it was the style; it never distributed her weight evenly and always made my back hurt. Maybe it hurt her, too. Maybe I should try one of those papoose thingies the happy mom was wearing. Not that I needed one right now or anything. But maybe someday.

    It might be good if our daughter had a sibling.

    Maybe . . .

THE END OF THE BEGINNING

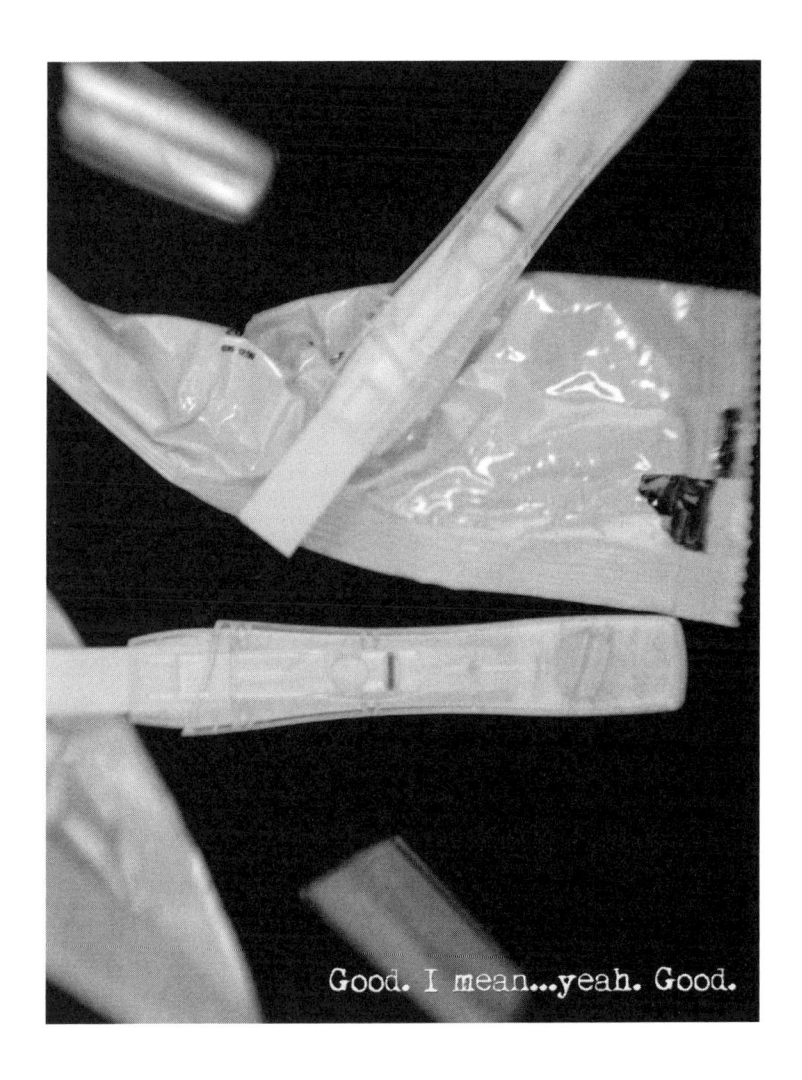

THE TOP 10 WARNING SIGNS THAT YOU MIGHT BE KNOCKED UP SOON

10.) You rub circles around your stomach, catch yourself, and continue as if it were normal, acceptable behavior. Your stomach flutters with the memory of secret changes.

9.) You "pass" a Babies"R"Us on the way home and stop in to "do some very early Christmas shopping." You get giddy as you feel the soft layette for the opposite sex, and inspect the really cool baby things that weren't around when you last gave birth.

8.) You do a mental inventory of the baby items you have in the basement, versus the ones you still haven't gotten back from friends. When did they become such hoarders? And why were you so eager to lend out your expensive stuff in the first place?

7.) A store employee catches you sniffing a bottle of Johnson & Johnson baby wash.

6.) You remember how much you *loved* food after you gave birth. Everything tasted good. The inside of your mouth salivates at the memory of Mom's leftover pasta when the sauce had time to soak in the flavor of the cheese and meat.

5.) Ahhhh, breast-feeding. It was so romantic. And natural.

4.) You swing violently back and forth between, "Ahhhh! This is so exciting," and, "Are we crazy?"

THE END OF THE BEGINNING

3.) You flip through all of your first child's baby pictures again. Awwww. Remember when you had to raise the mattress to the highest level in the crib? And when she slept through everything? And when opening her neck rolls was like going on a treasure hunt? Everything was so teeny tiny: the onesies, the blankies, the diapers, the hats, the nail clippers. . . .

2.) You fool yourself into believing that the already-existing child will be excited and helpful and loving and understanding by day 4 of being a "new family." When you picture how you'll convalesce, you remember only the meals other people prepared for you last time and the hours you slept in the middle of the day.

1.) Somehow, even with all of your experience, you're already scribbling baby name combinations because you've forgotten everything.

Dummy.

SANITY
LINGERING

ACT NOW CK OR SAY
GOOD-BYE TO LINGERING SANITY

Dear CK,

Unless you renew now, your LINGERING SANITY subscription faces termination.

But there is one last chance for you to keep your SANITY coming without interruption – and that is by acting now, while your subscription is still active.

It's not too late to avoid conception and we here at LINGERING SANITY would like to remind you of the mental, physical and financial cost of DECEMBER, **just one month brought on by your first lapse in SANITY.**

CHILD ONE: Conjunctivitis, stomach virus, ear infection, and staph infection. $736 in office visits, antibiotics, eye drops, carpet cleaners, Pedialyte, bribery treats, day care paid for but not attended and Sesame Street Band-Aids.

YOU: Stomach virus, viral infection and four nights without sleep leading to dizziness, exhaustion, attitude and the fear of pregnancy. Loss of 28 hours of sick time. $141 in office visits, Excedrin, Robitussin with codeine, and pregnancy tests.

So act now and cash in on nights of sleep, relative quiet and vomit-free fashion.

Don't make the same mistake twice, CK. Return the Last Chance/Savings Certificate today.

Or say good-bye to the remains of your LINGERING SANITY.

Sincerely,

U.R. Sanity

U.R. Sanity
Consumer Marketing Director

▼ DETACH AND RETURN REORDER FORM IN ENCLOSED PREPAID REPLY ▼

LAST CHANCE/SAVINGS CERTIFICATE

YES! I want to save 71% off the cover price. Please renew me for the term indicated.
To receive and online order confirmation and other information, please provide your e-mail address.

MRS CK
N CAMAC STREET
PHILADELPHIA   PA 19107-0001

109765432100   ICTIAM GPHMDWI
↳ YOUR ACCOUNT NUMBER

CHOOSE ONE:
☐ 114 issues at $150 an issue
☐ 57 issues at $450 an issue

CHECK ONE:
☐ Payment enclosed
☐ Bill me later in full
☐ Bill me later in 3 monthly installments

PLEASE REORDER BY:
RIGHT/NOW/!
NowEXP

Printed in U.S.A.

To renew online, go to www.badmommymoments.com

I SHOT THE CHEVY

I locked the keys in my Cavalier again, right in the ignition. Third time this month. The first time I was at work, and the other two times I'd just returned home and parked in front of the house. I left the engine running all three times. Once I even left my daughter in the car. She was happy, and safe, and I couldn't get her out.

In other related doings, I ran out of the house twice, locked the door, and left the keys in the living room. I called my father-in-law for help after the first lockout, but after the second I was too embarrassed to call him, so I slipped in through the doggie door. Again.

Since I was too paranoid to hide keys in my yard, I decided it was time for a new line of defense each time I left the house, or exited the car:

1. Jingle the keys at least twice before closing the front door.
2. After parking the car, manually unlock the passenger-side door from the inside before removing the key from the ignition.
3. Jingle the keys at least twice while exiting the car.
4. Lock the driver-side door from the outside.
5. Jingle the keys at least twice while walking to the passenger side of the car to get the baby out.

My first attempt was a perfect, key-in-the-right-place success. I arrived at the day care, ran through the assault, and locked the driver-side door with confidence. I even jingled the keys to the melody of the song my daughter and I had been singing together in the car. *Sing what I sing, sing after me. Be my echo if you can be. Sing tra, la, la . . .*

And then the car rolled away.

BAD MOMMY MOMENTS

With my daughter still inside.

The keys were in my pocket, but I'd forgotten to put the car in park. I grabbed the driver-side door handle. The car kept rolling. I ran around the car and grabbed the bumper. The car kept rolling. I raced to the other side of the vehicle, yanked open the passenger-side door, and jumped in. The car kept rolling . . . right toward a shiny Navigator. I slammed on the brake and jerked the car into park. No one was hurt. What was wrong with my brain? The last time it lapsed like this . . .

THE END OF THE BEGINNING

EVOLUTION OF THE ANNOUNCEMENT

My husband's mother died when he was three. His last memory of her was on his third birthday when she handed him an Ernie doll with balloons. He held onto the Ernie doll until he was eleven and his half brother was born. On their first Christmas together, he gave Ernie to his little brother, along with a letter that explained that Ernie always made him feel safe, and he wanted his brother to feel safe, too. But someone accidentally threw Ernie away with the Christmas wrappings.

When my husband and I started contemplating kids, I went Ernie-shopping. Since his mom was an identical twin, and twins also ran in my family, I bought two dolls just to be safe. The morning I found out I was pregnant, my husband had already left for work. I spent the day in a dreamy haze. I hugged myself, touched my stomach, and gazed at the wall with a huge secret in my heart.

That night I gave him one of the Ernie dolls. He raised an eyebrow. I said it was for him to give to our baby so that he or she would always feel safe. And then I promised never to throw it out in the trash. We got teary-eyed, hugged, kissed, and took the dog for the first of many walks where we debated names, the baby's sex, and which one of us was the cuter kid growing up.

I shoved the second Ernie back into the closet where he remained for almost three years. Most of the time I didn't think about him, but every once in a while I remembered that he was in a corner of the house, struggling to breathe. In my heart I believed we'd have a need for that Ernie one day, I just couldn't fathom ever wanting that day to arrive. Until it did. Once again I found out that I was pregnant in the morning before work, only this time my husband was still home. I raced to the closet and started digging. My daughter's screams began as I located Ernie's arc of fuzzy hair, and by the time I pulled his stripes from the bag, she was pounding the walls.

"No! I wear this!" she screamed. I rushed down the stairs and found my daughter struggling to cover her nakedness with a raincoat, the outfit I'd dressed her in sopping up water in the dog's bowl.

"I wear this!" She jumped up and down.

My husband just shook his head at her. She raced into the living room and threw herself onto the couch. He looked up at me. His eyes were already a million miles away, sequestering his brain in a mental safe house.

And yet, here he was.

Here we both were.

What were we thinking?

I tossed the second Ernie at him. "You ready?"

He looked at the doll for a moment and laughed. Our eyes met. We smiled and stared down the long hallway where our naked daughter was slapping her raincoat on the floor.

Here we go....

Dear TWO,
Just a few requests while you gestate
(in order of importance):
1) Please want to cuddle.
2) Please sleep.
3) Please be easy; I need a break.
4) Please love your sister.
5) Please adore your daddy as much as I do.

Other than that, please feel free to be yourself.

NEXT TIME

PLEASE, PLEASE DON'T

Please don't . . .
. . . do that. I know you're just trying to help, but when you give your sister a hammer during her diaper change, everyone loses. Where did you find that, anyway?

Please don't . . .
. . . sit that way. If you want to wear a dress in the sandbox, you'll either have to cross your legs or sit on your knees. You're not for sale.

Please don't . . .
. . . run with a paintbrush in your mouth. Best case scenario, you don't fall and puncture the back of your throat, but you bite down on it and . . . well? What did you think would happen?

Please don't . . .
. . . eat a muffin while on the toilet. I shouldn't have to keep reminding you not to bring food in the bathroom. You're not there to picnic. *Focus.*

Please don't . . .
. . . kick the back of my seat. It makes my head pound and . . . *what did I just say?*

Please don't . . .
. . . play with plastic bags. Nothing good can come from walking around with a bag on your head.

BAD MOMMY MOMENTS

Please don't . . .

. . . scream like that when I drop you off at school. I lose approximately two minutes of my alone time to guilt when you do that. You go one day a week. Suck it up.

Please don't . . .

. . . resuscitate your gum after dropping it on the floor at Target. It's dead. There's nothing we can do.

Please don't . . .

. . . lick the bottom of your shoe. I'm trying to let you make your own decisions, but so far you're doing a lousy job.

Please don't . . .

. . . follow me in here. Can't I have one place? One minute? One thing that's mine? And mine because I choose it, not because you don't want it anymore?

No?
Fine.
Then hand me the hammer, close the door behind you, and be on your way.

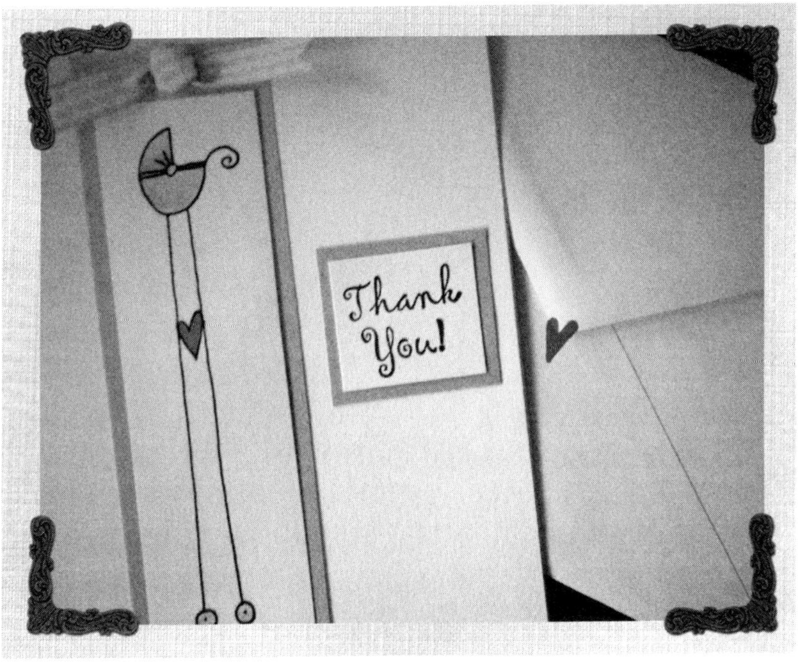
Thank
You!

ACKNOWLEDGMENTS

God: Thank You for who You are and how You've changed my life in the course of this book. Thank You for all of the artists You placed in my path to create what I could only envision. Most importantly, thank You for my family, and for teaching me through Your gentle and constant example how to meet their needs without losing myself.

My husband: Thank you for giving me the reasons to write this book, for being a sounding board for ideas, and for creating more than half of the graphics.

My daughters: Thank you for filling my days with the kind of chaos, angst, humor, and love it takes to create a book like this.

My family: Thank you for the love and respect you've always shown my dreams. Thank you for reading, supporting, and encouraging everything I've ever written, even the stuff that landed us in the counselor's office.

My amazing friend and editor, Christine Harkin: Thank you for your ideas, your instincts, and your investment in my work. Thank you for giving my 300-page dream a spine.

My writing partner, Brad Pettingell: Thank you for teaching me how to "unpack" my words and for helping me find my voice.

ARTISTS/CONTRIBUTORS

Illustrator/animator/graphic designer Steve Ellis (http://beautifulrust.net): I have so much to thank you for. Thank you for taking my words and creating *The Breast® Manual, Lingering Sanity, Fart Postcard, Lost, Please Ignore Me,* and *Mommything,* Thank you for your work on *Baby's First Lie, Cornucopia, Constipated, I Wish I Still Felt this Excited, Hiding Place,* and *Monday, Sunny Monday.* Thank you for always being a wonderful brother. I am so grateful for you.

Photographer Christine Zona (http://czona.com): Thank you for spending two years working with me cross-country on this project. Every time I look at your photographs I'm excited by the ways you captured my visions in *Cornucopia, Constipated, Lost, Origami Fortune Teller, Fart Postcard, Dear TWO,* the pregnancy test shots, and your images in the *I Wish I Still Felt This Excited* composite graphic.

Website designer Sarah Fite (http://sarahfitedesigns.com): Thank you for telling me the format of my old blog sucked and that it hurt your eyes to read. Your vision breathed life into my site.

Sarah Melville: Thank you for living through every stage of this book with me; I would've been lost without you. Speaking of *Lost,* thanks for lending your double-Ds for page 45. Only the truest BFF would offer her breasts when the cleavage meant to star in the graphic regressed to the beginning of the alphabet. (And many thanks to Adam Molaver for his photographic prowess in terms of said breasts.)

ACKNOWLEDGMENTS

Graphic artist Kendra McCarrick (http://spanstylestudios.com): Thank you for the *Getting Started* and *Using Breasts®* layout and for your patience every time the text needed revisions.

Fine artist Rita Coffern: Thank you for your delicate work on *Baby's First Lie*.

Jen Adams (Pink Tulip Cards): Thank you for your beautiful *Thank You* cards.

Faith Goodiel: Thank you for sharing your *Origami Fortune Teller* skills.

Lori Kartman (http://isuloribell.blogspot.com): Thank you for submitting your shower photo for the *I Wish I Still Felt This Excited* composite graphic.

Rhea Coffern: Thank you for going through the revised text and cleaning it up on behalf of the objectivity I no longer possessed.

Dana Talusani (http://thekitchwitch.com): Thank you for your fantastic notes on my manuscript, and for sharing your "ugly baby" photograph for *Baby's First Lie* (though we all know Miss M turned out to be the most gorgeous child on the planet).

Thanks to my wonderful friends who submitted themselves to focus groups and gave me fantastic notes: Liza Draper (http://pacifiersanonymous.com), Jen Miller, Lindsay Guzman, Alissa Gapinski, Shelia O'Grady, Liz Talotta, Erica Watson, Laura Hogan, Kathy Belinski, Molly Crismond, Jackie Madusky, MaryAnne Haskell, and Jill Mellott.

ACKNOWLEDGMENTS

Thanks to Mark Levine, Michelle Brown, Kate Ankofski, Hannah Lee, Kristeen Ott, Brenda Rathje, Danielle Adelman, and Sheryl Trittin of Two Harbors Press.

And finally, I want to thank each person who visits my blog and reads this book. Thank you for sharing your time, your hearts, and your experiences with me. Motherhood is much less daunting when you're surrounded by people who laugh with you, and accept you as you are.

ABOUT THE AUTHOR

Photo courtesy of Grace Brown

Cindy Kane is a graduate of the Writing for Film and Television program of the University of the Arts in Philadelphia. She currently blogs at badmommymoments.com, and performs her stories with SpeakeasyDC (speakeasydc.org).

Cindy lives in Virginia with her husband, two daughters, and Maggie, the golden retriever who neither swims nor retrieves.